CB078502

Pathway to Math 3

Student's Book

Glue your picture here.

Name

Richmond

Richmond
58 St Aldates
Oxford
OX1 1ST
United Kingdom

Pathway to Math Student's Book Level 3

First Edition: March 2016
First Reprint: March 2017
ISBN: 978-607-06-1257-2

Pathway to Math 3 is a collaborative work, created and designed by the Department of Educational Research of Santillana. Richmond adapted the project and created an English version.

Av. Río Mixcoac No. 274, Col. Acacias,
Benito Juárez, C.P. 03240, Ciudad de México

Publisher: Justine Piekarowicz
Editorial Team: Catalina Hernández, Natalia Herrera, Duncan Jones, Jacaranda Ruiz, Milosh Trnka
Pre-Press Coordinator: Daniel Santillán
Cover Design: Lourdes Arroyo

Cover Photograph: ©THINKSTOCK: (Ingram Publishing)

Illustrations: Martín Oyarce Gallardo

Photographs: Archivo Santillana
©THINKSTOCK: iStock pp. 25, 39, 55, 61, 75, 85, 95, 117, 137, 147 (graphic-bee), 25, 39, 55, 61, 75, 85, 95, 117, 137, 147 (luctra_design).

Printed in Brazil by Forma Certa Gráfica Digital
Lote: 794434
Cod: 292712572

Introduction

Hi friends!

We are **Spot**  and **Kiki**  and we are here to welcome you to **Pathway to Math**. Follow us on the Pathway to Math, where learning becomes special. Do you want to know why?

- This pathway is full of magic, and everyone is welcome on it. You will find information, texts, pictures and activities presented in a simple and friendly manner. Here you will discover that learning is fun!
- This is a pathway where we can all learn to share and live together. The activities will help us reflect on our values and learn to respect others.

- This is a pathway open to people from all over the world where you can learn interactively with the help of the latest technology.
- This is a pathway full of challenges that involve finding solutions, developing math skills and applying calculation strategies that you and your classmates will work on together.

We will be with you every step of the way!
All you need is curiosity and the desire to learn.

How is your textbook organized?

Pathway to Math 3 is organized into five units. Here is what you will find in each unit.

Initial Pages

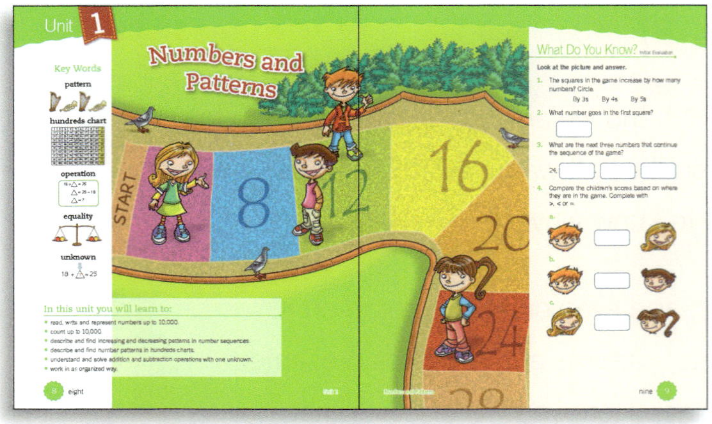

- Number and title of the unit
- Learning objectives
- Initial evaluation

Sections Organized by Learning Objectives

- Let's Connect
- Let's Learn
- Let's Practice
- Quiz Yourself

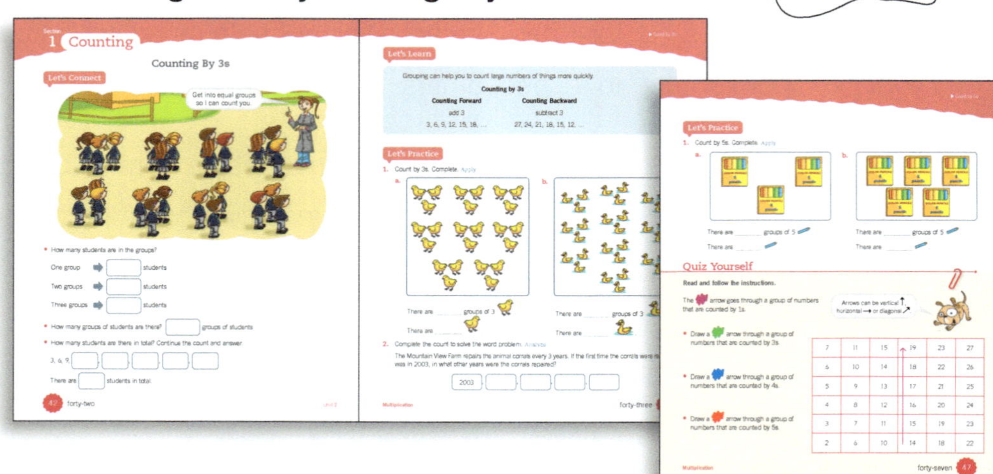

Fun Features

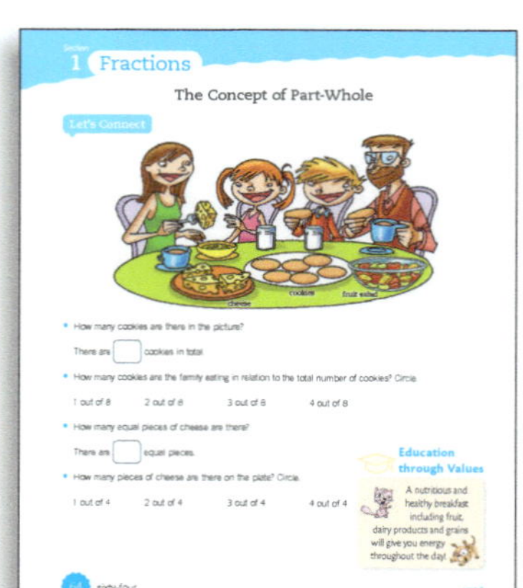

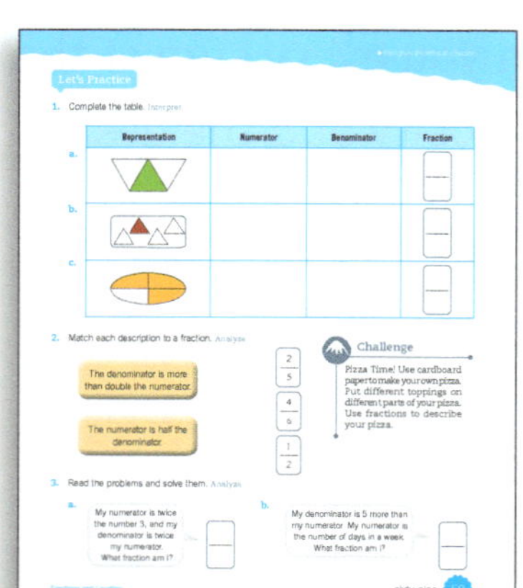

- Education through Values
- Did You Know...?
- Remember
- Tip
- Word Focus
- Fun Fact!
- Challenge

Evaluation Pages

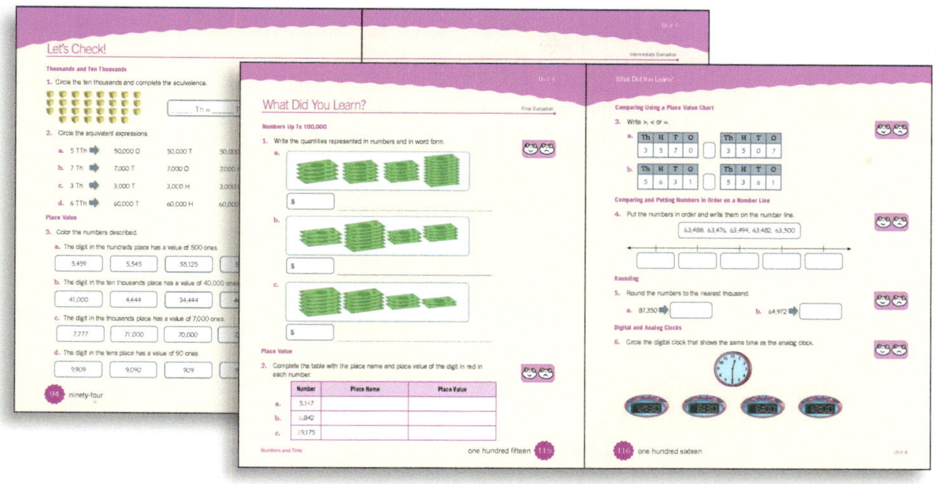

- What Do You Know?
  Initial Evaluation
- Let's Check!
  Intermediate Evaluation
- What Did You Learn?
  Final Evaluation

Special Pages

- Exam Strategies
- Test Study Pages
  Summary and Review

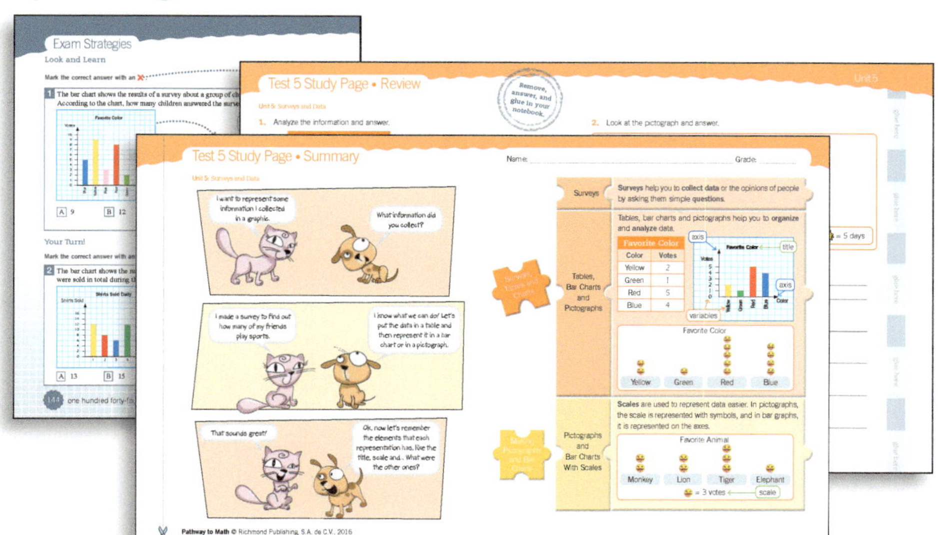

Support Pages

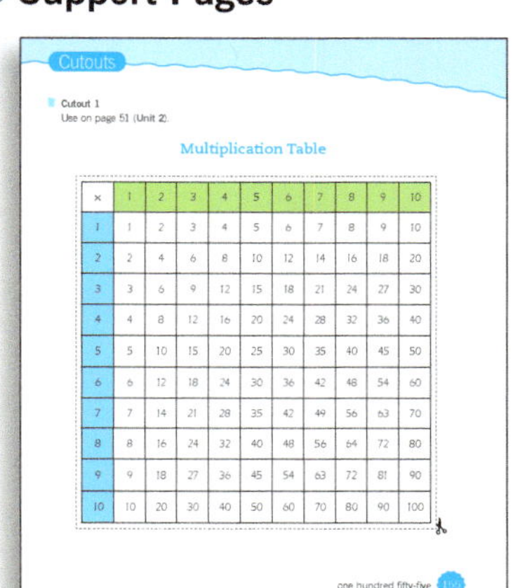

- Cutouts

Table of Contents

Unit 1

Numbers and Patterns

Key Words

pattern

hundreds chart

1	2	3	4	5	6	7	8	9	10
11	12	13	14	15	16	17	18	19	20
21	22	23	24	25	26	27	28	29	30
31	32	33	34	35	36	37	38	39	40
41	42	43	44	45	46	47	48	49	50
51	52	53	54	55	56	57	58	59	60
61	62	63	64	65	66	67	68	69	70
71	72	73	74	75	76	77	78	79	80
81	82	83	84	85	86	87	88	89	90
91	92	93	94	95	96	97	98	99	100

operation

$18 + \triangle = 25$

$\triangle = 25 - 18$

$\triangle = 7$

equality

unknown

$18 + \triangle = 25$ (the △ contains "?")

In this unit you will learn to:

- read, write and represent numbers up to 10,000.
- count up to 10,000.
- describe and find increasing and decreasing patterns in number sequences.
- describe and find number patterns in hundreds charts.
- understand and solve addition and subtraction operations with one unknown.
- work in an organized way.

What Do You Know? Initial Evaluation

Look at the picture and answer.

1. The squares in the game increase by how many numbers? Circle.

   By 3s By 4s By 5s

2. What number goes in the first square?

   [ ]

3. What are the next three numbers that continue the sequence of the game?

   28, [ ], [ ], [ ]

4. Compare the children's scores based on where they are in the game. Complete with >, < or =.

   a.  [ ] 

   b.  [ ] 

   c.  [ ] 

Section 1

Numbers Up To 10,000

Reading and Representing Numbers Up To 10,000

Let's Connect

The third grade visited the Modern Art Gallery with their teacher.

- How many paintings are there?

  There are ☐ paintings.

- How much does the cheapest painting cost? Write the price in word form.

  ____

- How much does the most expensive painting cost? Write the price in word form.

  ____

Let's Learn

When you read and represent a number you have to consider how many digits it has.

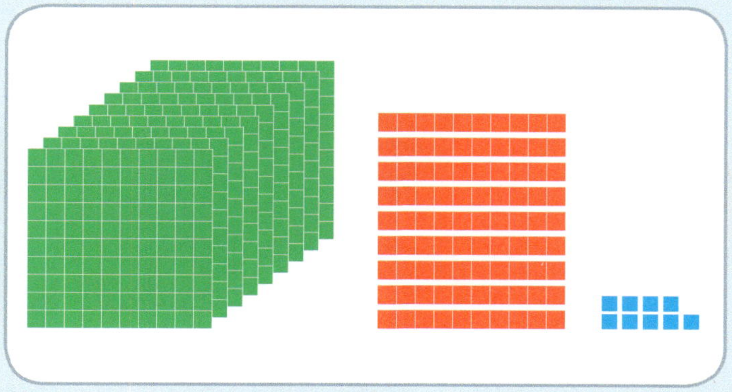

999
nine hundred ninety-nine

Add the word "thousand" and a comma after the fourth digit, from right to left.
When you read numbers in the thousands, say the word "thousand" where the comma is.

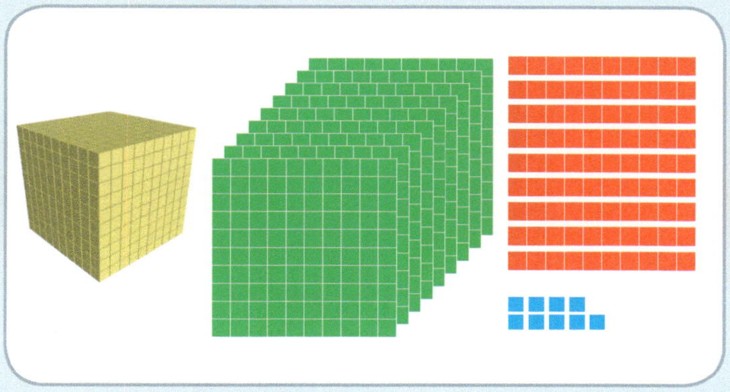

1,999
one thousand, nine hundred ninety-nine

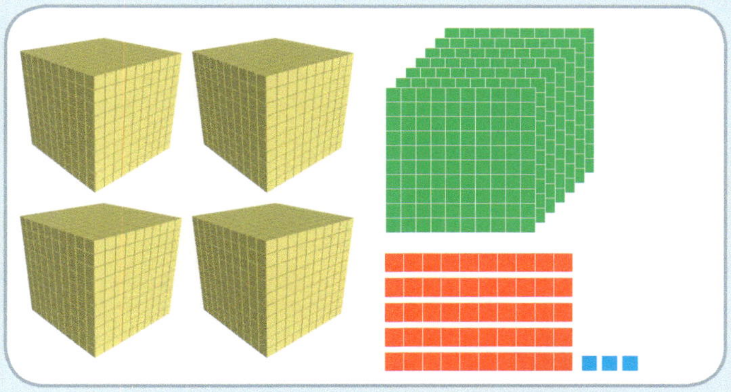

4,753
four thousand, seven hundred fifty-three

Let's Practice

1. Write the numbers represented. Represent

a.

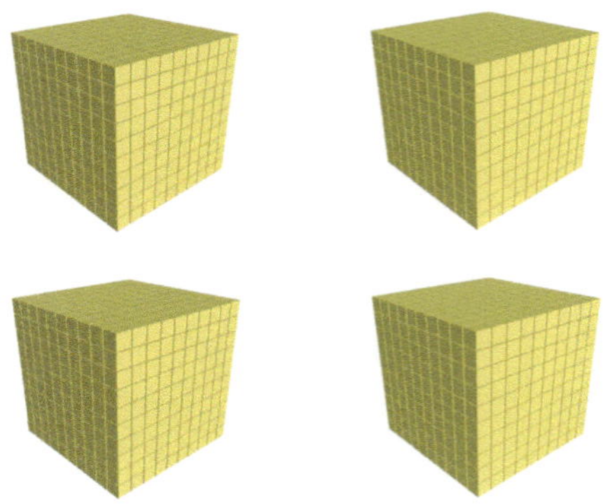

b.

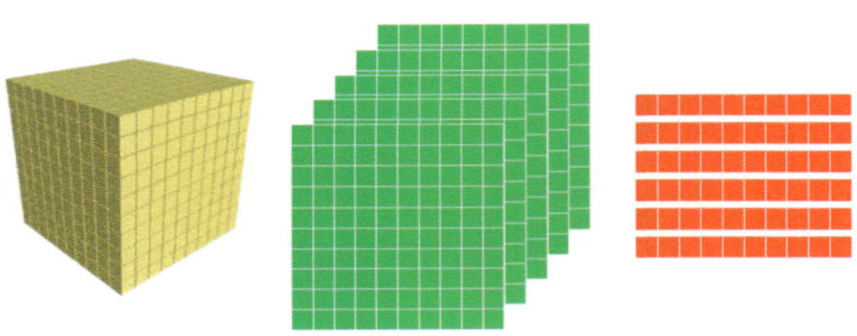

c.

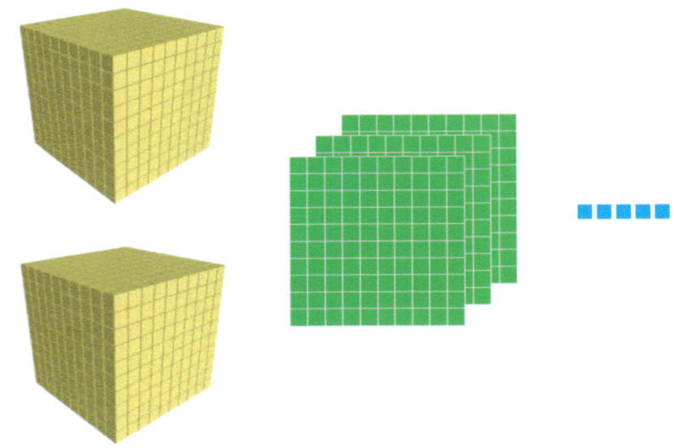

d.

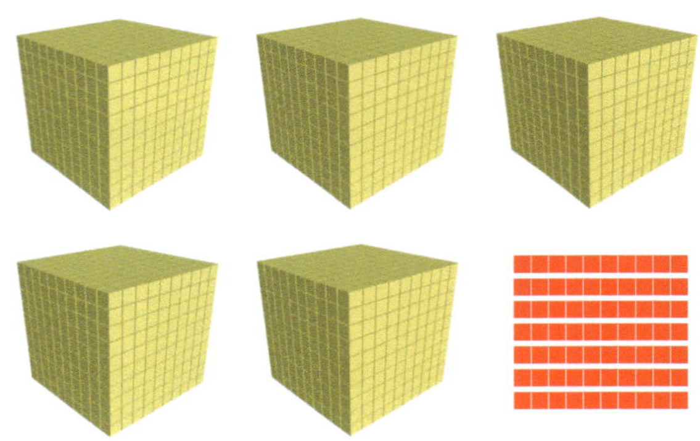

Did You Know...?

The Romans used capital letters to represent numbers.

Roman Numeral System	I	V	X	L	C	D	M
Decimal Numeral System	1	5	10	50	100	500	1,000

All numbers can be represented by combining Roman numerals. Numbers 1 to 10 are written I, II, III, IV, V, VI, VII, VIII, IX, X.

2. Write the numbers represented in word form. Represent

a.

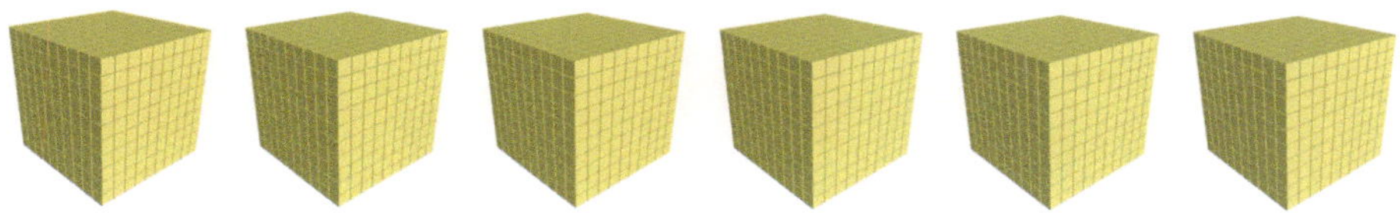

____

b.

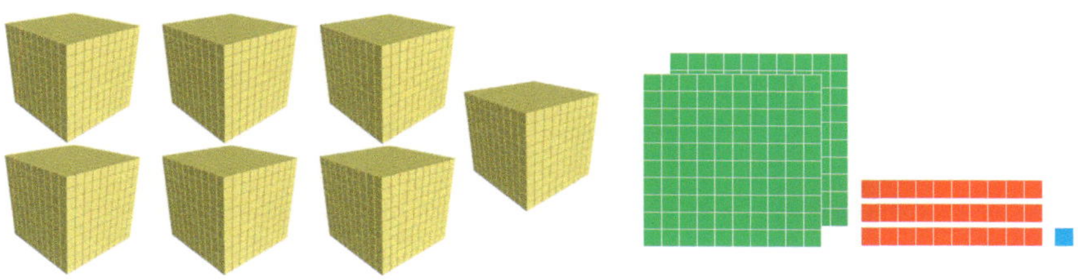

____

c.

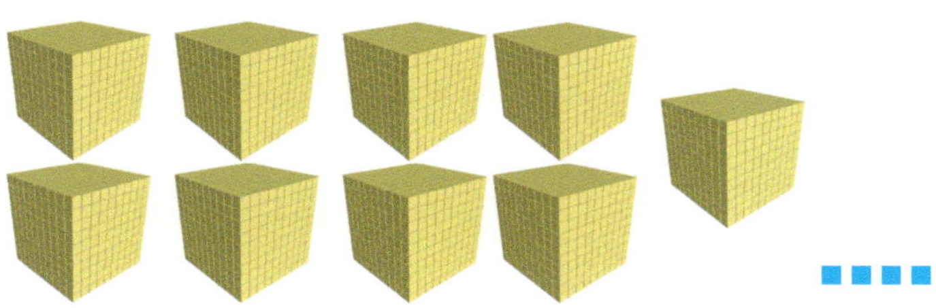

____

d.

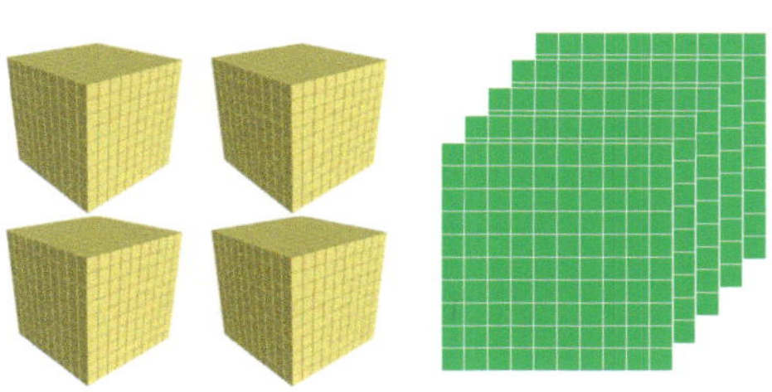

____

3. Use the key to represent the numbers. Represent

 = 1  = 10  = 100  = 1,000

a. 983

b. 3,240

c. 2,031

d. 7,305

4. Write the numbers in word form. Represent

a. 7,000 ➡ ____________________

b. 2,896 ➡ ____________________

c. 5,540 ➡ ____________________

d. 6,489 ➡ ____________________

e. 9,090 ➡ ____________________

5. Write the numbers. Represent

a. nine thousand ➡ [ ]

b. four thousand, one hundred thirty-eight ➡ [ ]

c. one thousand, four hundred four ➡ [ ]

d. seven thousand, seventy-two ➡ [ ]

e. nine thousand, nine hundred ninety-nine ➡ [ ]

Remember!

Use a comma between the thousands and the hundreds places.
E.g. 3,456
T,H

6. Write the year you were born in numbers and in word form. Apply

[ ]

____

Counting

Let's Connect

1,100	1,101	1,102	1,103	1,104	1,105	1,106	1,107	1,108	1,109
1,110	1,111	1,112	1,113	1,114	1,115	1,116	1,117	1,118	1,119
1,120	1,121	1,122	1,123	1,124	1,125	1,126	1,127	1,128	1,129

- You start counting from number ☐.
- How many numbers does the count increase by each time? Answer.

____

- Look at the highlighted numbers in the table. What other numbers should be highlighted? Answer.

____

Let's Learn

- Count by **5s**, starting from any number. ➡ 1,101, 1,106, 1,111, 1,116, 1,121, ...
- Count by **10s**, starting from any number. ➡ 1,119, 1,129, 1,139, 1,149, 1,159, ...
- Count by **100s**, starting from any number. ➡ 1,245, 1,345, 1,445, 1,545, 1,645, ...

Let's Practice

1. Continue the number sequences. Apply

- By 5s.

a. 1,250, ____, ____, ____, ____, ____, ____

b. 2,511, ____, ____, ____, ____, ____, ____

- By 10s.

c. 2,321, ____, ____, ____, ____, ____, ____

d. 7,001, ____, ____, ____, ____, ____, ____

- By 100s.

e. 4,520, ____, ____, ____, ____, ____, ____

f. 9,022, ____, ____, ____, ____, ____, ____

Quiz Yourself

The symbols represent numbers:

 = 1

 = 10

 = 100

 = 1,000

- Identify the pattern. Write how much the count increases by each time.

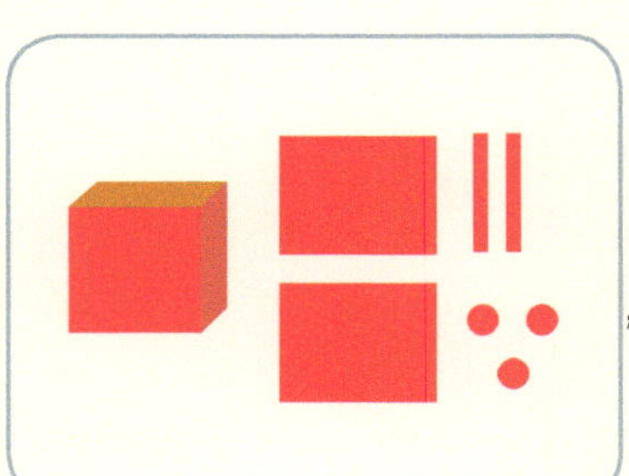, 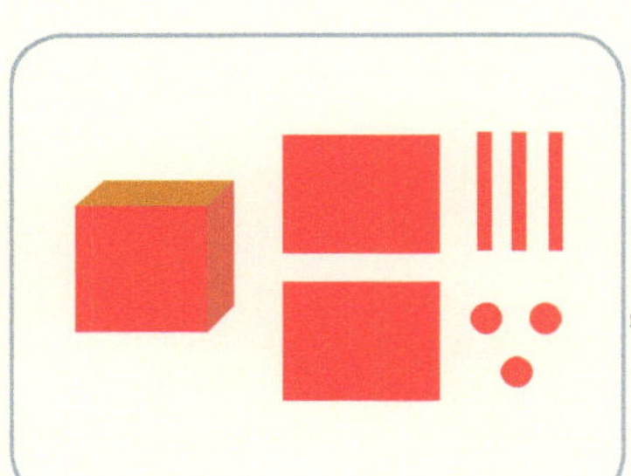, 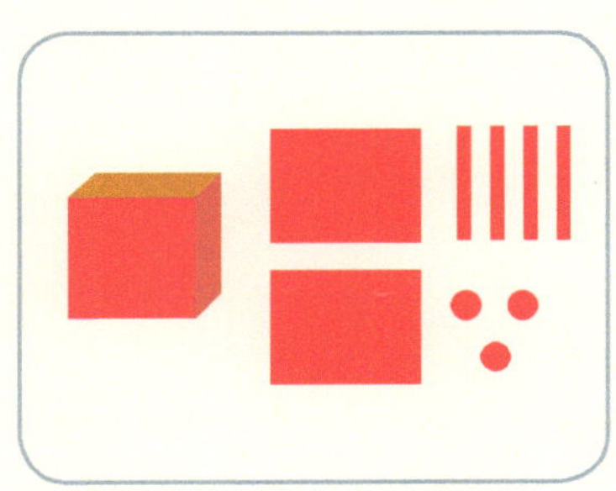 ____

Section 2

Number Patterns

Increasing and Decreasing Patterns

Let's Connect

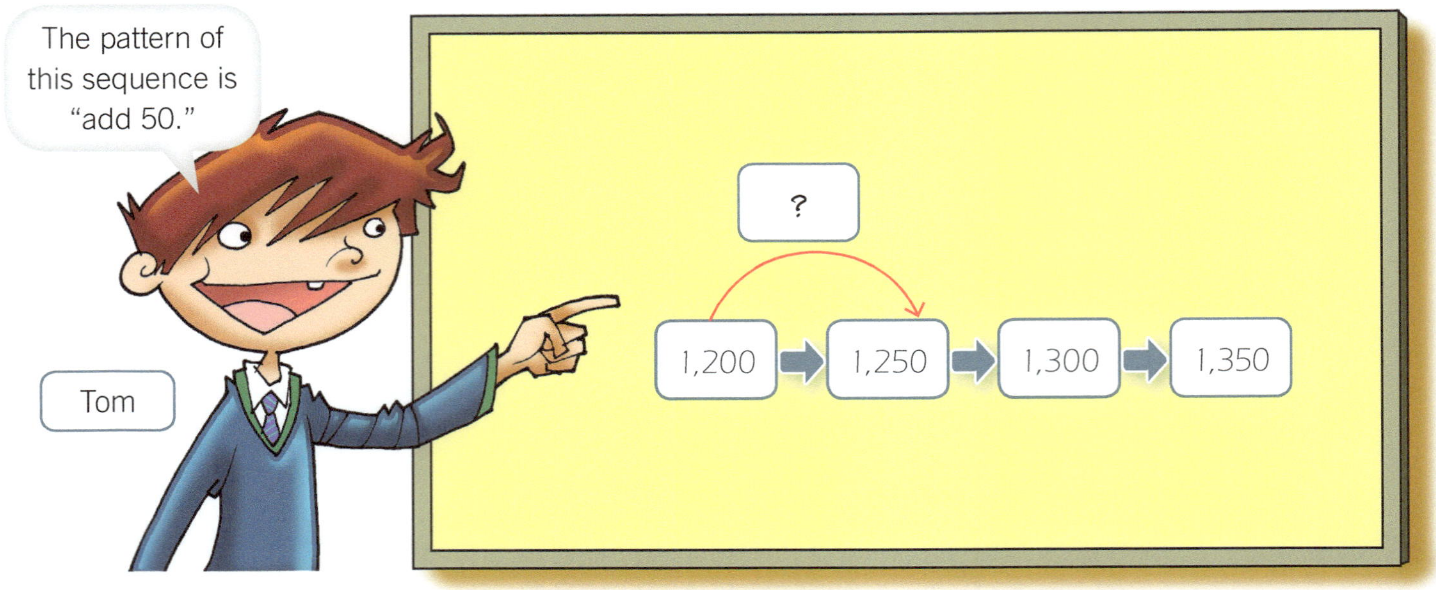

- Is the number sequence increasing or decreasing? Write your answer and explain.

____

- What are the differences between these numbers? Calculate and write them.

1,250 and 1,200 → 1,250 – 1,200 = ☐

1,300 and 1,250 → 1,300 – 1,250 = ☐

1,350 and 1,300 → 1,350 – 1,300 = ☐

Remember!

A **pattern** is a repeating arrangement of numbers, colors or shapes.

- Is Tom's statement correct? Why? Answer.

____

____

____

Let's Learn

To recognize and describe a **pattern** for a number sequence, first identify if the direction of the sequence is **increasing** and going forward or **decreasing** and going backward.

Increasing	Decreasing
Each term in a sequence is **less than** the one that follows. **Addition** is used between terms.	Each term in a sequence is **greater than** the one that follows. **Subtraction** is used between terms.
1,200 → 1,250 → 1,300 → 1,350	1,350 → 1,300 → 1,250 → 1,200

Then **identify the number added to or subtracted from** the term. To do this, find the difference between two **consecutive** terms. Repeat this process with the other terms in the number sequence to check if the pattern is the same.

Number Sequence: 1,200 → 1,250 → 1,300 → 1,350

1,250 – 1,200 = 1,300 – 1,250 = 1,350 – 1,300

Pattern: add 50 or + 50

Let's Practice

1. Write the pattern for each sequence. Apply

a. [ ]

3,330 ➡ 3,334 ➡ 3,338 ➡ 3,342 ➡ 3,346 ➡ 3,350

b. [ ]

15,845 ➡ 15,745 ➡ 15,645 ➡ 15,545 ➡ 15,445 ➡ 15,345

Number Patterns in a Hundreds Chart

Let's Connect

1	2	3	4	5	6	7	8	9	10
11	12	13	14	15	16	17	18	19	20
21	22	23	24	25	26	27	28	29	30
31	32	33	34	35	36	37	38	39	40
41	42	43	44	45	46	47	48	49	50

- What is the pattern of the numbers in (green)?

1 → 2 → 3 → 4 → 5 → 6 → 7 → 8 → 9

- What is the pattern of the numbers in (yellow)?

10 → 20 → 30 → 40 → 50

- What are the patterns for the digits in the ones places and in the tens places of the numbers in (blue)?

Pattern for digits in the ones place: ____________________

Pattern for digits in the tens place: ____________________

Remember!

A **number sequence** always has an order and follows a pattern.

Let's Learn

You can find different patterns in a hundreds chart if you look at the numbers **horizontally**, **vertically** and **diagonally**.

1	2	3	4	5	6	7	8	9	10
11	12	13	14	15	16	17	18	19	20
21	22	23	24	25	26	27	28	29	30
31	32	33	34	35	36	37	38	39	40
41	42	43	44	45	46	47	48	49	50
51	52	53	54	55	56	57	58	59	60
61	62	63	64	65	66	67	68	69	70
71	72	73	74	75	76	77	78	79	80
81	82	83	84	85	86	87	88	89	90
91	92	93	94	95	96	97	98	99	100

For example:

- the pattern for the yellow column is **add 10** (+10).
- in the tens column, the digit in the tens place **increases by 1** and the digit in the ones place is **always zero**.

Let's Practice

1. Look at the hundreds chart. Write a number sequence from the chart and describe its pattern. Understand

a. ☐ → ☐ → ☐ → ☐ → ☐ → ☐ → ☐ → ☐ → ☐

Pattern of digits in the ones place: ____________________

Pattern of digits in the tens place: ____________________

2. Color the chart. Understand

a. A row that has a pattern of add 1 (+1).

b. A column that has a pattern of add 10 (+10).

c. A diagonal that has a pattern of add 11 (+11).

1	2	3	4	5	6	7	8	9	10
11	12	13	14	15	16	17	18	19	20
21	22	23	24	25	26	27	28	29	30
31	32	33	34	35	36	37	38	39	40
41	42	43	44	45	46	47	48	49	50
51	52	53	54	55	56	57	58	59	60
61	62	63	64	65	66	67	68	69	70
71	72	73	74	75	76	77	78	79	80
81	82	83	84	85	86	87	88	89	90
91	92	93	94	95	96	97	98	99	100

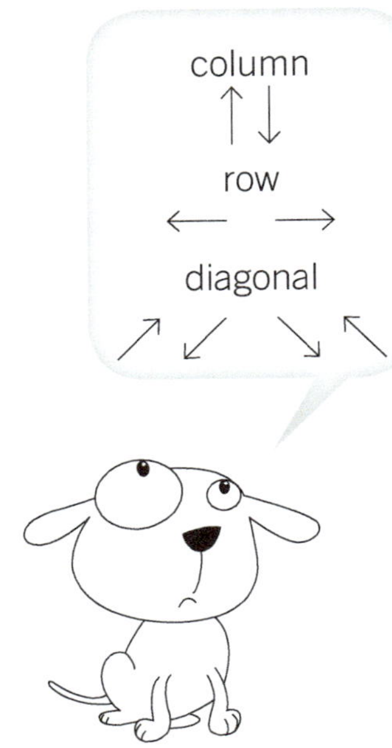

3. Using the hundreds chart above, write **T** for **true** and **F** for **false**. Explain. Evaluate

a. ☐ In all diagonals, the digit in the ones place and the tens place increases by 1.

____

b. ☐ In all columns, the digit in the ones place stays the same.

____

c. ☐ All columns, from top to bottom, have a pattern of add 10 (+ 10).

____

d. ☐ All rows, from left to right, have a pattern of add 10 (+ 10).

____

4. Work out the patterns and complete the hundreds charts. Infer

a.

21	22	23	24
	42		

b.

			55
		64	
	73		

5. Write the unknown number that follows in each sequence. Infer

a.

44			
	55		
		?	

▶ [ ]

b.

		38	39
	47	48	
?			

▶ [ ]

6. Look at the sequences in the multiplication tables and find the patterns. Analyze

a.

	x10
1	10
2	20
3	30
4	40
5	50
6	60
7	70
8	80
9	90

Pattern ▶ [ ]

b.

	x9
1	9
2	18
3	27
4	36
5	45
6	54
7	63
8	72
9	81

Pattern ▶ [ ]

Let's Check!

Number Patterns

1. Write the pattern for each number sequence.

a. [ ]

2,214 ➡ 2,221 ➡ 2,228 ➡ 2,235 ➡ 2,242

b. [ ]

10,516 ➡ 10,510 ➡ 10,504 ➡ 10,498 ➡ 10,492

c. [ ]

24,301 ➡ 24,311 ➡ 24,321 ➡ 24,331 ➡ 24,341

2. Use the patterns to continue the number sequences.

a. + 20

2,300 ➡ [ ] ➡ [ ] ➡ [ ] ➡ [ ]

b. – 1,500

15,600 ➡ [ ] ➡ [ ] ➡ [ ] ➡ [ ]

Number Patterns in a Hundreds Chart

3. The tables are parts of a hundreds chart. Complete them.

a.

		35	
43			

b.

1			
			24

c.

	12		
	32		

d.

	82		
		93	

4. Write **T** for **true** and **F** for **false** for the information about hundreds charts. Explain.

a. ☐ The pattern of all rows is add 1.

____

b. ☐ The pattern of all columns is add 11.

____

How Did You Do?

For each frog face color a lily pad.

Operations With One Unknown

Let's Connect

Did You Know...?

We use the symbols < and > to express **less than** or **more than**.

$5 < 7$

five is **less than** 7

$7 > 5$

seven is **more than** 5

- What is the relationship between the quantities on each side of the scale? Mark your answer with a ✓.

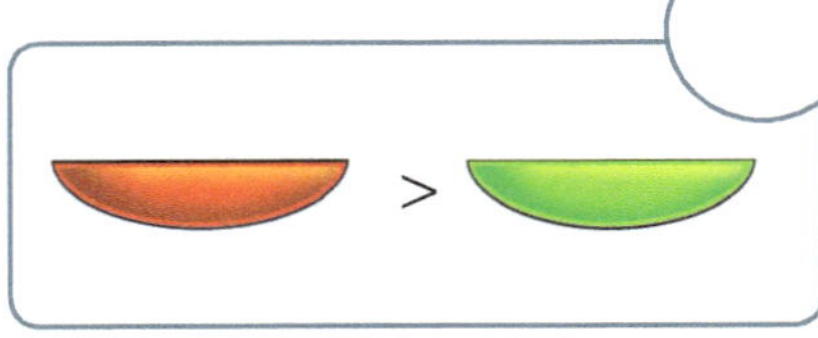

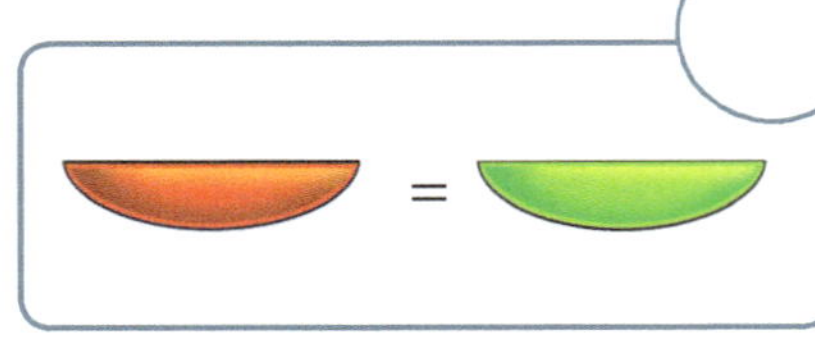

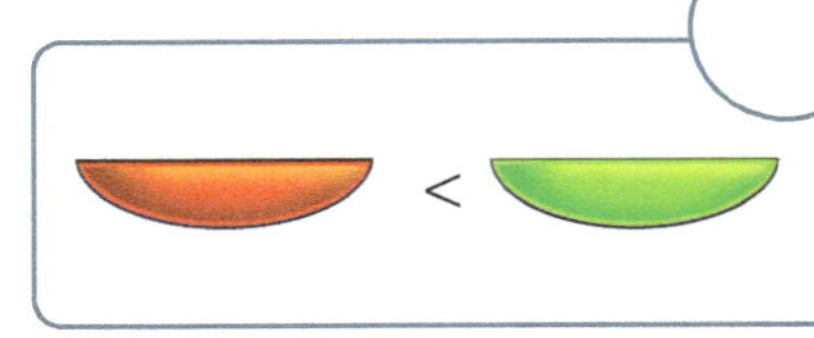

- Which operation represents the weights on the scale? Circle it.

13 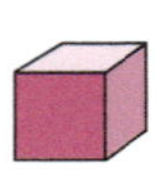 −  = 17 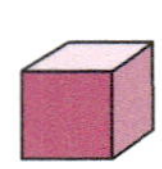

13 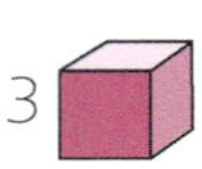 +  = 17 

- How many blocks need to be in the  for the scale to be balanced? Calculate and answer.

There are ☐ blocks in the  .

Let's Learn

A **balanced** scale can represent an operation that has **known values** and an **unknown value**.

13 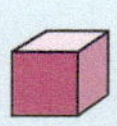 plus the 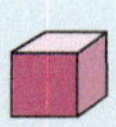 in the  equals 17 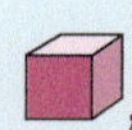, since the scale is balanced. This means:

13 +  = 17

Therefore,  represents the **unknown value**.

Did You Know...?

An **unknown** can be represented by a symbol, such as a geometric shape.

13 + 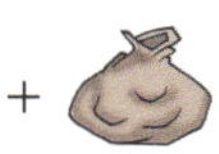 = 17

↓

13 + △ = 17

Challenge

Draw a hundreds chart. Then give your partner clues like "this number is 5 times 3" or "this number is 50 plus 7." Your partner marks the numbers on his or her table using the clues. Then switch roles.

Let's Practice

1. Circle the operations with unknown values. Understand

26 − 14 = 12

26 − △ = 12

40 + 1 = 41

□ + 19 = 32

8 + ○ = 17

13 + 19 = 32

45 − 10 = 35

31 − ? = 3

2. Mark the operation represented by each scale with a ✔. Interpret

a.

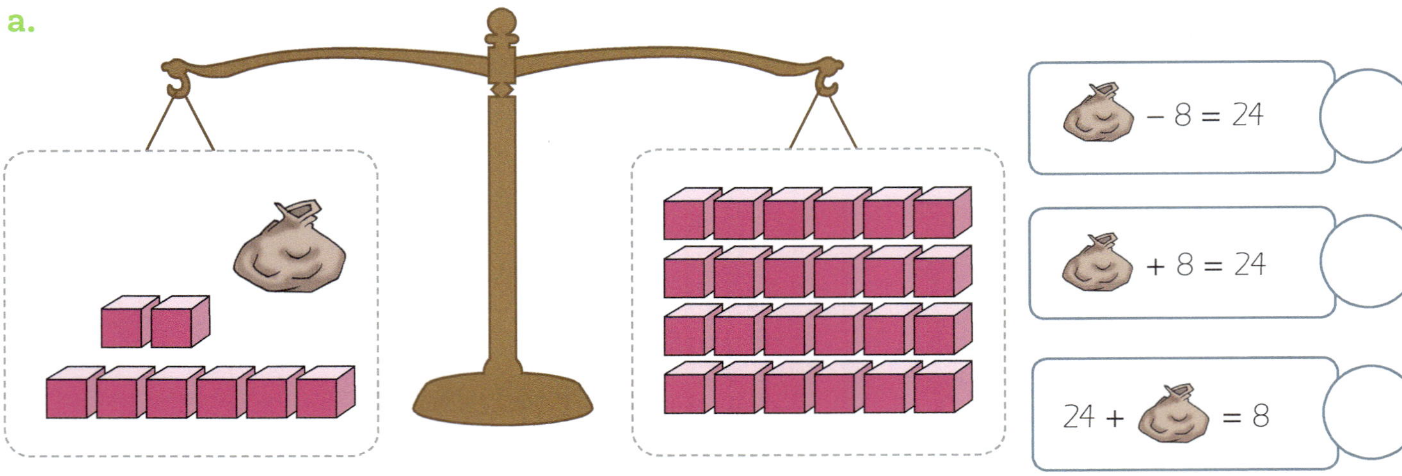

b.

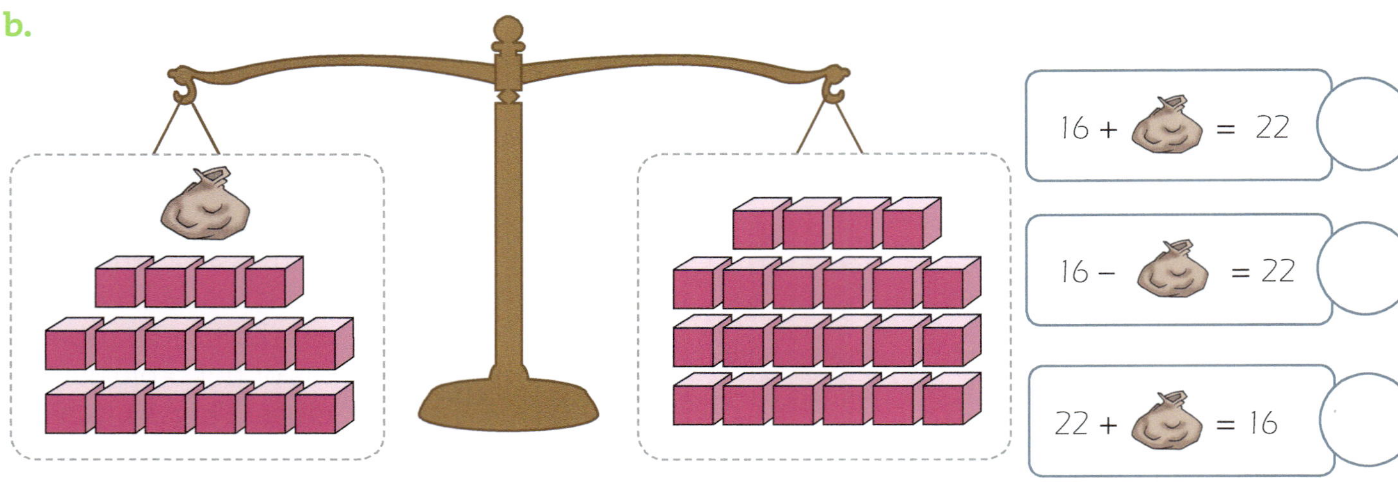

c.

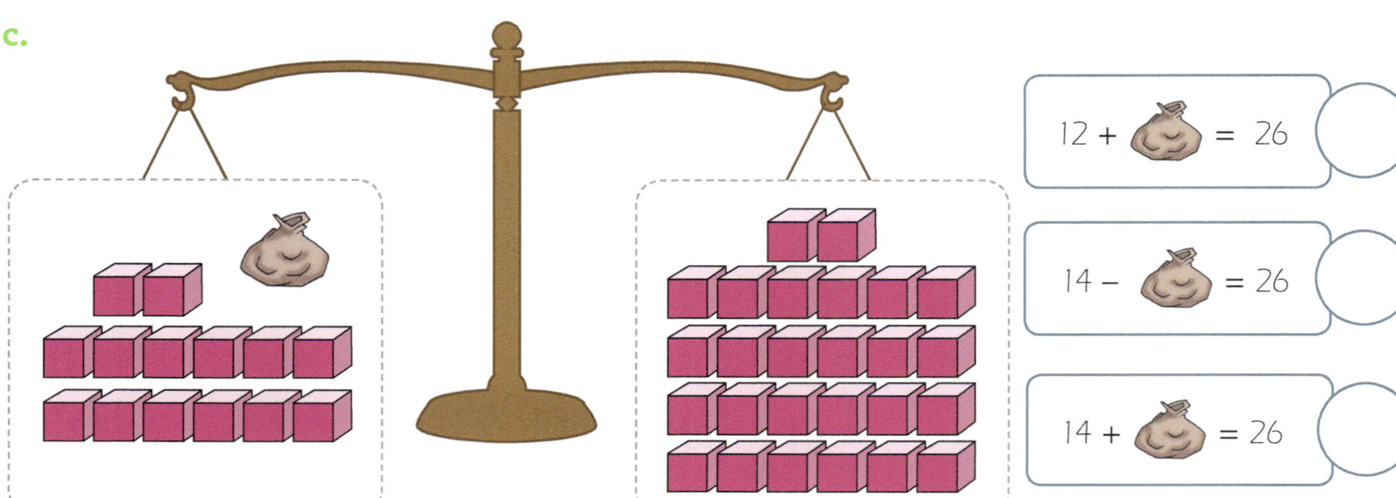

3. Represent each operation by drawing ◯. Represent

a. 12 + △ = 18

b. 22 + □ = 30

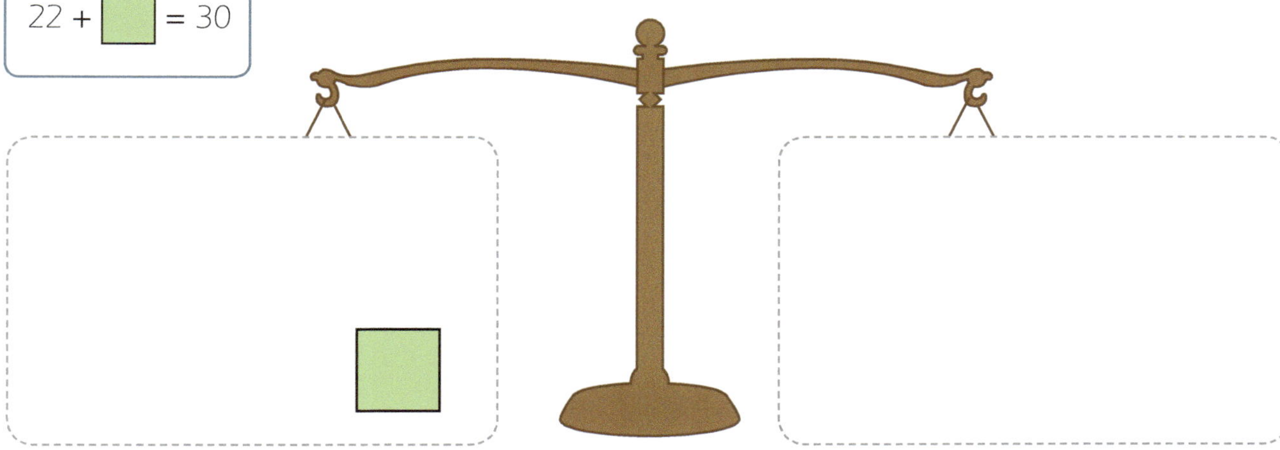

c. ⬡ + 10 = 25

Addition Operations With One Unknown

Let's Check

- How many blocks are on the ? Write your answer.

  There are ☐ blocks.

- How many blocks are on the ? Circle your answer.

  18 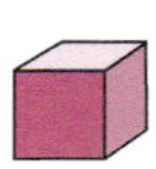 +    18 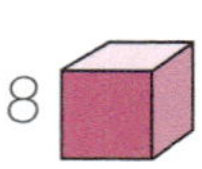 − 

- Which operation represents the scale? Circle it.

  18 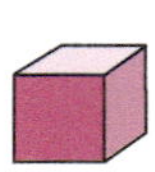 + △ = 25 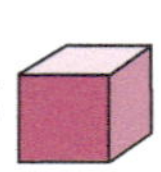   25 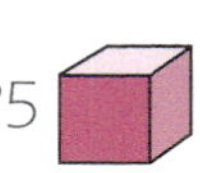 + △ = 18 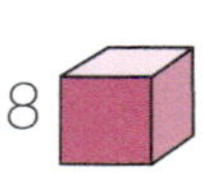

- What value should △ have to make both sides of the scale equal? Answer and explain.

The value of △ is ☐.

Let's Learn

Any situation with an **unknown** can be represented by an **equality**.

$$18 + \triangle = 25$$

An **addition** operation can be solved by:

- representing the operation.

- relating the addition operation to its inverse operation, **subtraction**.

$$18 + \triangle = 25$$
$$\triangle = 25 - 18$$
$$\triangle = 7$$

Let's Practice

1. Write the operation that represents each scale. Represent

a.

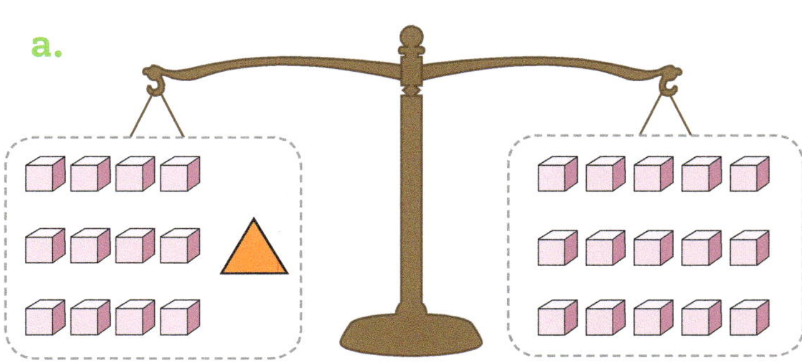

b.

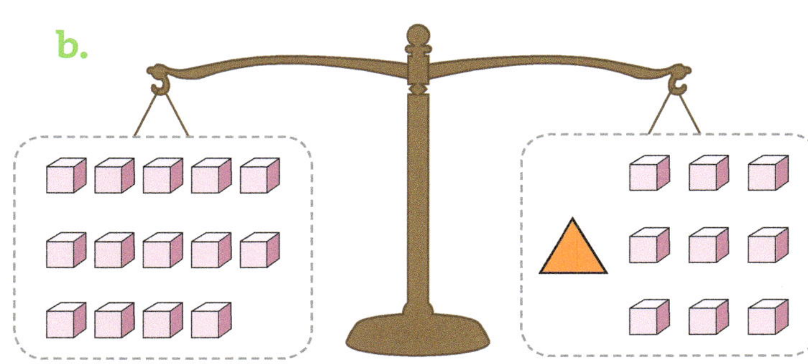

2. Write the operations. Then calculate the values of the unknowns and write them. Apply

a.

 +  = 

Operation: ______ Value of the unknown = ______

b.

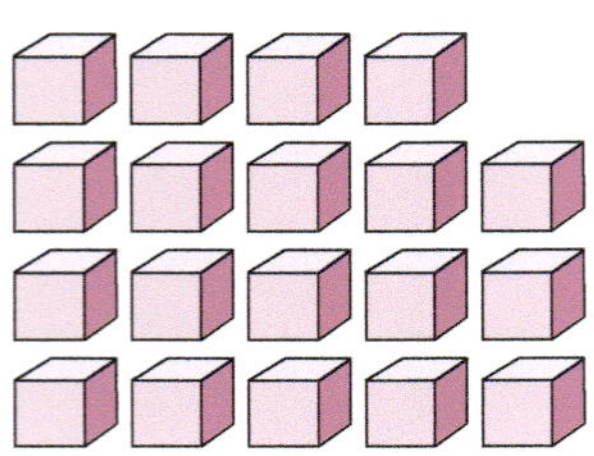 +  = 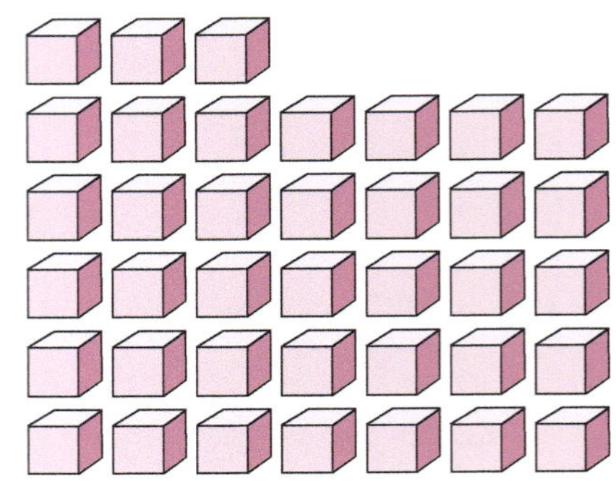

Operation: ______ Value of the unknown = ______

3. Solve the operations. Apply

a. 24 + △ = 45

c. □ + 23 = 55

b. ○ + 17 = 34

d. 31 + ⬡ = 58

Remember, you can use different symbols to represent an **unknown**.

4. Solve each word problem by following the steps.

a. Sandra and Jeffrey have to collect 50 milk cartons each. Jeffrey has 28 and Sandra has 50. How many more cartons does Jeffrey need to collect?

Write the operation that represents the problem. ▶

Solve the operation to find the unknown value.

Write the value of the unknown. ▶

Answer ▶ ______________________________

b. Noah put identical pencils on both sides of the scale. There are 33 pencils on one tray and 22 on the other. How many pencils does Noah need to put on the tray with fewer pencils for the scale to be balanced?

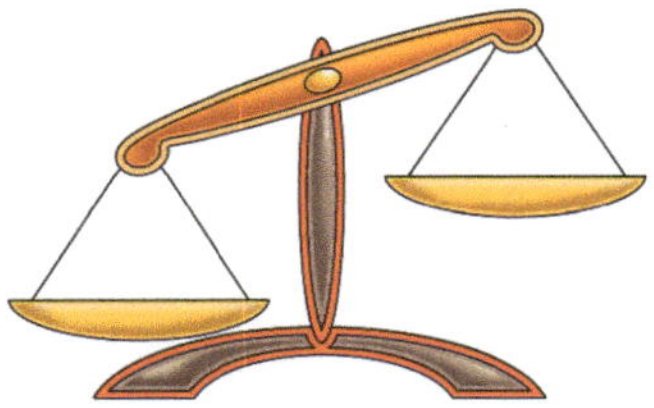

Write the operation that represents the problem. ▶

Solve the operation to find the unknown value.

Write the value of the unknown. ▶

Answer ▶ ______________________________

Subtraction Operations With One Unknown

Let's Connect

How many blocks were on the left tray if the scale is balanced when I remove 7 blocks?

- How many blocks are there on the ?

  There are ☐ blocks.

- How many blocks did Jess remove from the ?

  She took away ☐ blocks.

- Which operation represents the scale? Circle it.

  △ − 7 = 20   20 − △ = 7

- What is the value of △? Answer and explain.

Remember that addition is the inverse operation of subtraction.

The value of △ is ☐.

Let's Learn

Any situation with an **unknown** can be represented by an **equality**.

△ − 7 = 20

A **subtraction operation** can be solved by:

- representing the operation.

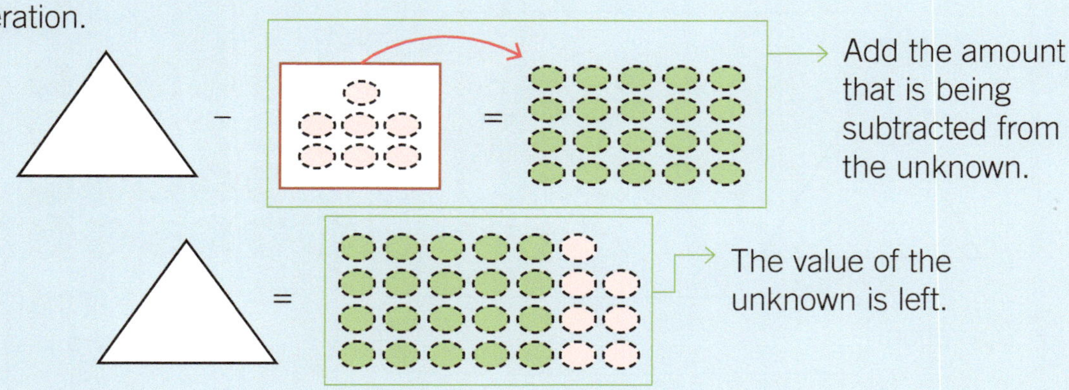

- relating the subtraction operation to its inverse operation, **addition**.

△ − 7 = 20
△ = 20 + 7
△ = 27

Let's Practice

1. Write the operation represented by each scale after removing the blocks. Represent

a.

b.

2. Write the operations. Then calculate the values of the unknowns and write them. Apply

a.

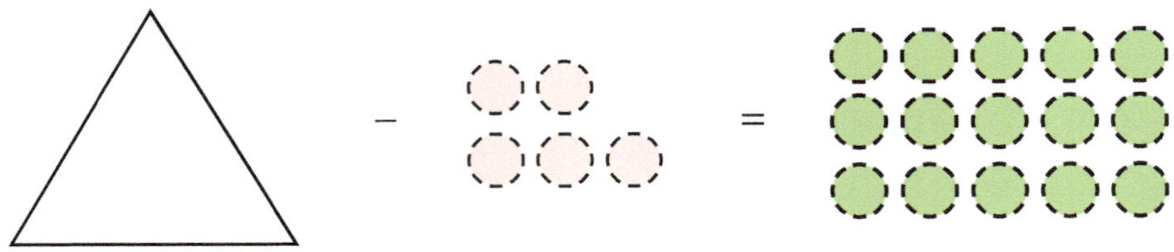

Operation:

Value of the unknown =

b.

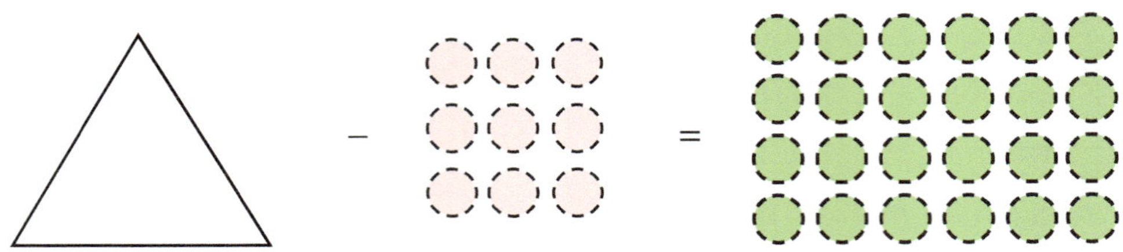

Operation:

Value of the unknown =

3. Solve the operations. Apply

a. △ − 48 = 24

b. ⬡ − 33 = 25

c. □ − 18 = 10

d. ○ − 15 = 28

Exam Strategies

Look and Learn

Mark the correct answer with an ✗.

Read the instructions carefully.

1 To balance a scale, Liz removed 12 balls from the right tray. If the left tray has 42 balls, how many balls did the right tray originally have?

- A 30
- ☒ B 54
- C 42

Read and understand the problem. In this case, to find the unknown value, you can write or represent the operation.

Analyze the choices and mark the correct answer with an ✗. Check your answer to be sure.

Your Turn!

Mark the correct answer with an ✗.

2 Lena wants to balance a scale. If she has 28 balls on one side and 14 on the other, how many balls does she need to add?

- A 14
- B 42
- C 28

What Did You Learn?

Numbers Up To 10,000

1. Write the quantities represented in numbers.

a.

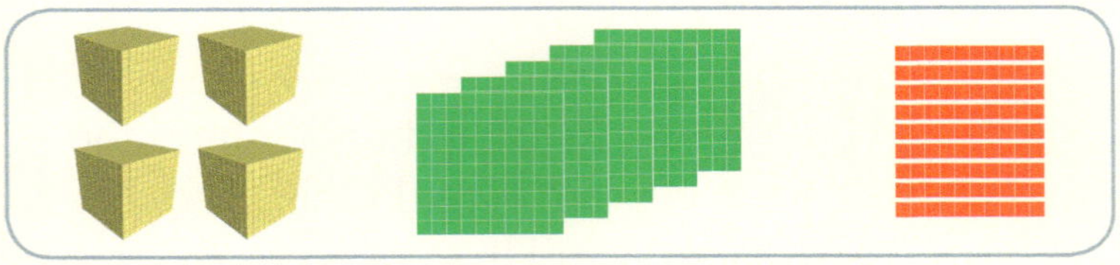

____

b.

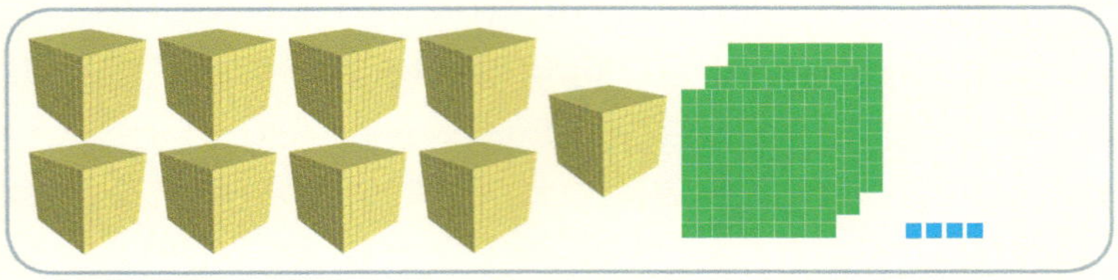

____

Number Patterns

2. Find the patterns and continue the sequences.

a.

[ ]

3,268 → 3,278 → 3,288 → [ ] → [ ]

b.

[ ]

6,709 → 6,609 → 6,509 → [ ] → [ ]

Number Patterns in Hundreds Charts

3. What are the numbers that follow the pattern in each hundreds chart? Write them in the colored squares.

a.

	?		39
?		48	
		?	

[ ] [ ] [ ]

b.

13			?
		25	
?			?

[ ] [ ] [ ]

Mark the correct answer with an ✕ .

Use the picture to answer questions 4–6.

4. Which operation with one unknown represents the scale?

A △ – 18 = 46

B 18 + △ = 46

C 46 + △ = 18

5. Which operation solves the problem?

A 46 + 18 = △

B 18 + 46 = △

C 46 – 18 = △

6. What is the value of the unknown?

A 28

B 64

C 18

Find Test 1 Study Page

How Did You Do?

For each 🐸 color a ⬭.

Multiplication

Key Words

grouping

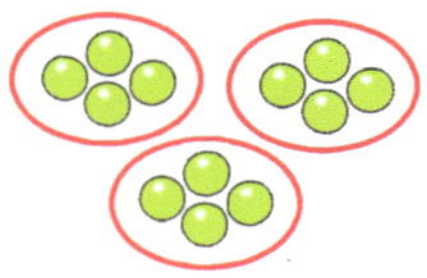

equal distribution

multiplication terms

factors → 3 × 4 ; product → 12

$3 \times 4 = 12$

repeated elements

3 + 3 + 3
4 + 4 + 4
5 + 5 + 5

In this unit you will learn to:

- count by 3s, 4s and 5s.
- understand and express multiplication as repeated addition.
- understand and express multiplication with equal distribution.
- understand multiplication situations where one corresponds to many.
- solve multiplication word problems.

What Do You Know? Initial Evaluation

Look at the picture and answer.

1. How much do tickets to enter the farm cost? Write the amounts in word form.

   Adults: ______________________________

   Children: ____________________________

2. How much do two adult tickets cost?

3. How much does the father spend, in total, on tickets for his three daughters?

4. The mother brought apples to share during the trip. If she brought 1 apple for each of the children and 2 for each of the adults, how many did she bring in total?

Counting By 3s

Let's Connect

- How many students are in the groups?

One group ➡ ☐ students

Two groups ➡ ☐ students

Three groups ➡ ☐ students

- How many groups of students are there? ☐ groups of students
- How many students are there in total? Continue the count and answer.

3, 6, 9, ☐, ☐, ☐, ☐, ☐

There are ☐ students in total.

Let's Learn

Grouping can help you to count large numbers of things more quickly.

Counting by 3s

Counting Forward	**Counting Backward**
add 3	subtract 3
3, 6, 9, 12, 15, 18, …	27, 24, 21, 18, 15, 12, …

Let's Practice

1. Count by 3s. Complete. Apply

a.

There are ______ groups of 3  .

There are ______  .

b.

There are ______ groups of 3  .

There are ______  .

2. Complete the count to solve the word problem. Analyze

The Mountain View Farm repairs the animal corrals every 3 years. If the first time the corrals were repaired was in 2003, in what other years were the corrals repaired?

2003, ______, ______, ______, ______

Counting By 4s

Let's Connect

- How many yogurts are in each pack? Each pack has ☐ yogurts.
- How many packs of yogurts are there? There are ☐ packs of yogurts.
- How many yogurts are there in total? Follow the count to complete. Answer.

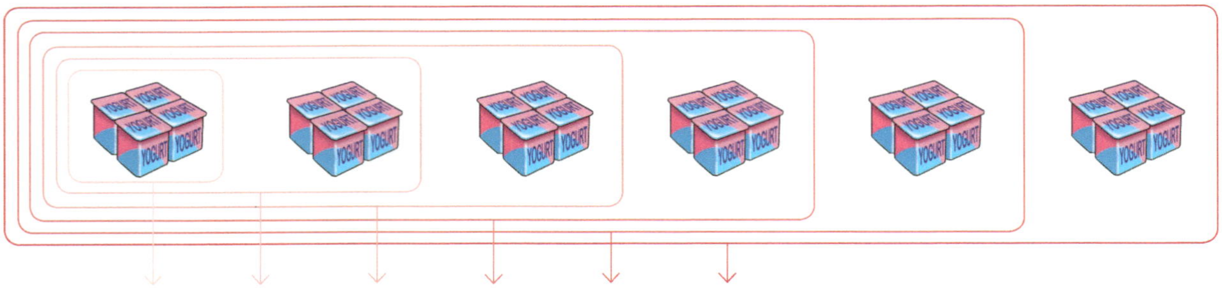

4, 8, ☐, ☐, ☐, ☐

There are ☐ yogurts in total.

Fun Fact!

The word *yogurt* comes from the Turkish word "to thicken." Yogurt was discovered in the Middle East over 4,500 years ago!

Education through Values

Choose nutritious and healthy snacks, like fruit, seeds and nuts. They will provide you with the necessary nutrients for proper development and you will grow up to be strong and healthy!

Let's Learn

Counting in groups that have the same number of elements can help you to count large numbers of things more easily.

Counting by 4s

Counting Forward	**Counting Backward**
add 4	subtract 4
4, 8, 12, 16, 20, 24, …	36, 32, 28, 24, 20, 16, …

Let's Practice

1. Count by 4s. Complete. Apply

a.

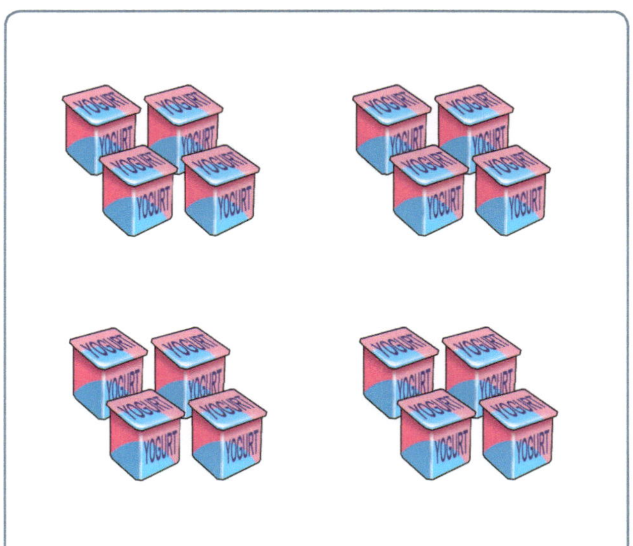

There are ________ groups of  .

There are ________  .

b.

There are ________ groups of  .

There are ________  .

2. Complete the count to solve the word problem. Analyze

There is a leap year every four years. If 2016 was the last leap year, what other years will be leap years?

2016, ______, ______, ______, ______

Did You Know...?

A leap year has 366 days instead of 365, because in a leap year the month of February has 29 days instead of 28.

Counting By 5s

Let's Connect

- How many groups of students are waiting to enter the feeding area?

  ☐ groups of students

- How many students are in each group?

  ☐ students

- How many students are there in total? Continue the count and answer.

  5, 10, ☐, ☐, ☐, ☐

  There are ☐ students in total.

Challenge

Challenge a friend to a skip counting contest. Who can count the highest by 3s? By 5s? Who can count the fastest without making a mistake?

Let's Learn

Grouping by 5s is a common way of quickly finding the total number of elements in a group.

Counting by 5s

Counting Forward	**Counting Backward**
add 5	subtract 5
5, 10, 15, 20, …	55, 50, 45, 40, …

Let's Practice

1. Count by 5s. Complete. Apply

a.

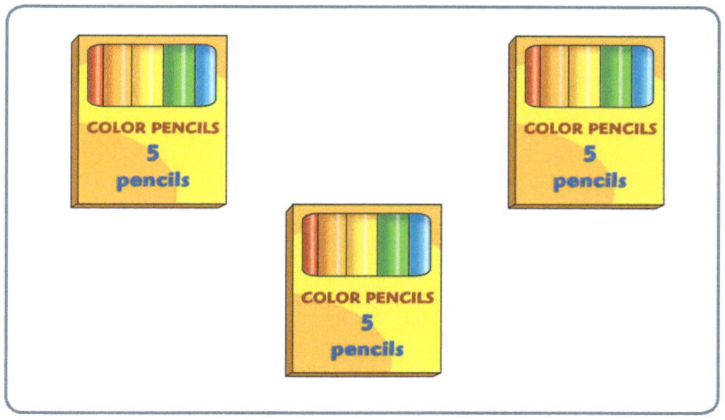

There are ________ groups of 5 .

There are ________ .

b.

There are ________ groups of 5 .

There are ________ .

Quiz Yourself

Read and follow the instructions.

The arrow goes through a group of numbers that are counted by 1s.

Arrows can be vertical ↑, horizontal ⟶ or diagonal ↗.

- Draw a arrow through a group of numbers that are counted by 3s.
- Draw a arrow through a group of numbers that are counted by 4s.
- Draw a arrow through a group of numbers that are counted by 5s.

7	11	15	19	23	27
6	10	14	18	22	26
5	9	13	17	21	25
4	8	12	16	20	24
3	7	11	15	19	23
2	6	10	14	18	22

Section

2 Multiplication

The Relationship Between Addition and Multiplication

Let's Connect

- How many flowers does each flowerpot have?

 ➔ ☐  ➔ ☐  ➔ ☐

- Which operation solves how many flowers there are in total? Circle.

addition subtraction

- Which expression represents the total number of flowers? Circle.

$4 + 4 + 4$ $3 + 3 + 3$

- How many times is the same number added to find the total number of flowers? Complete.

I added ☐ ☐ times.

- How many flowers are there in total?

There are ☐ flowers in total.

Let's Learn

An **addition operation with equal addends**, or **repeated addition**, can be represented as a multiplication operation.

4 + 4 + 4 = 12

3 times 4 is 12

$3 \times 4 = 12$

Tip

The terms of a multiplication operation are:

factors product

$3 \times 4 = 12$

multiplication sign

The × sign means multiplication and we say it as "times."

Let's Practice

1. Look at the pictures. Complete. Apply

a.

☐ + ☐ = ☐

☐ times ☐ is ☐

☐ × ☐ = ☐

b.

☐ + ☐ + ☐ = ☐

☐ times ☐ is ☐

☐ × ☐ = ☐

2. Match the expressions that are the same. Relate

3 + 3	4 + 4 + 4 + 4	3 + 3 + 3	6 + 6 + 6 + 6
2 × 3	4 × 6	3 × 3	4 × 4

Equal Distribution

Let's Connect

- How many hens are there? ☐
- How many eggs did each hen lay? ☐
- Which repeated addition operation represents this situation? Circle.

4 + 4 + 4 + 4 + 4   5 + 5 + 5 + 5

Let's Learn

When you have **groups** with the **same number of elements**, the total number of elements can be found using **multiplication**.

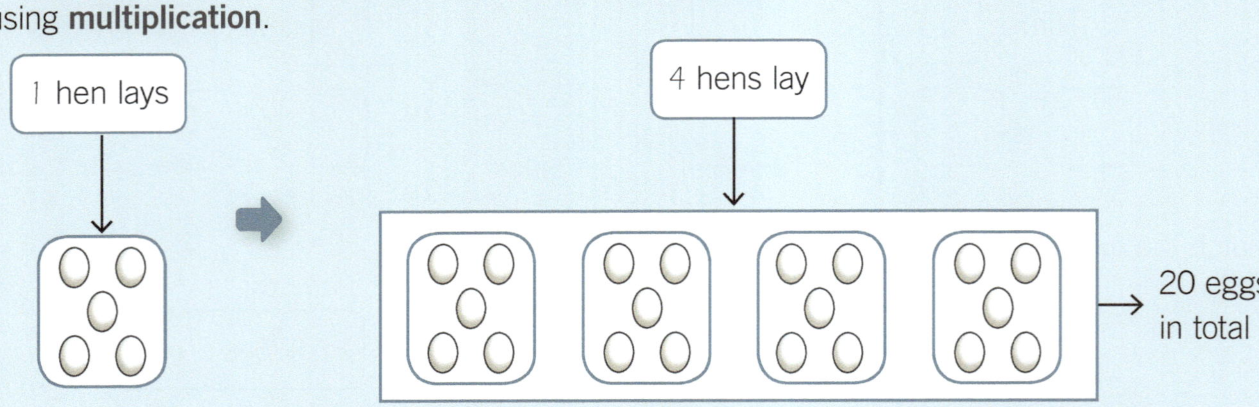

5 + 5 + 5 + 5 = 20
4 times 5 is 20
$4 \times 5 = 20$

Let's Practice

1. Match each situation with its representation. Relate

- I have 2 trays with 8 apples on each one.
- There are 4 corrals with 2 horses in each one.
- I have 8 bags with 2 marbles in each one.
- I have 2 vases with 4 flowers in each one.

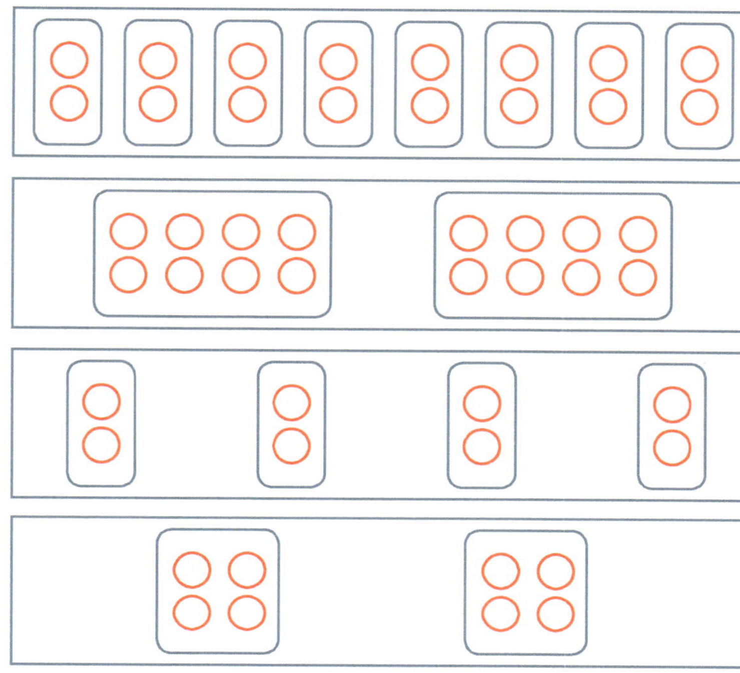

2. Represent each situation with a multiplication operation. Apply

a. Matt has 2 boxes to put his toys in. If he puts 8 toys in each box, how many toys will he put away in total?

➡
___ + ___ = ___
___ times ___ is ___
___ × ___ = ___

b. Anna and 3 friends offer to bring juice to share with the class. If each of them brings 4 bottles of juice, how many bottles of juice will they bring in total?

➡
___ + ___ + ___ + ___ = ___
___ times ___ is ___
___ × ___ = ___

2 times 1 is 2, **2 times 2 is 4**, **2 times 3 is 6**.
I have learned my 2s, 3s and 4s multiplication tables. Have you? Use the multiplication table from **Cutout 1** on **page 155** to learn them.

One Corresponding to Many

Let's Connect

- How many pens are there? There are ☐ pens.
- How many sheep fit in each pen? ☐ sheep fit in each pen.
- If there were 6 sheep in each pen, which repeated addition operation would represent the situation? Circle.

6 + 6 + 6 + 6   4 + 4 + 4 + 4 + 4 + 4

Let's Learn

When the number of elements of one group, for example, 1 pen, is equal to the number of elements in a second group, for example, 6 sheep, you can find the total number of elements in a third group, for example, 4 pens, by multiplying the number of elements in the second group (6 sheep), by the quantity you have of the first group (4).

Group 1		Group 2
1 pen	➡	6 sheep
2 pens	➡	12 sheep
3 pens	➡	18 sheep
4 pens	➡	24 sheep

$6 + 6 + 6 + 6 = 24$

4 times 6 is 24

$4 \times 6 = 24$

Let's Practice

1. Read each situation. Complete. Understand

a. Danielle reads 6 pages a day. How many pages will she read in 5 days?

➡

1 day	2 days	3 days	4 days	5 days

b. Mark works 9 hours a day. How many hours will he work in 5 days?

➡

1 day	2 days	3 days	4 days	5 days

2. Write the multiplication operation for each situation. Apply

a. When you complete a level in a videogame, you earn 3 points. If Andy has passed 6 levels, how many points does he have?

1st level	2nd level	3rd level	4th level	5th level	6th level

☐ times ☐ is ☐

$\square \times \square = \square$

b. If Leo takes his dog to the veterinarian 2 times a month, how many times will he take his dog to the veterinarian in 6 months?

1 month	2 months	3 months	4 months	5 months	6 months

☐ times ☐ is ☐

$\square \times \square = \square$

Let's Check!

Count by 3s, 4s and 5s

1. Count and complete.

a.

There are ______ groups of 6  .

There are ______  .

b.

There are ______ groups of 5  .

There are ______  .

Relating Addition and Multiplication

2. Write the multiplication operations. Then, solve them.

a. 3 + 3 ➡ ☐ × ☐ = ☐

b. 4 + 4 ➡ ☐ × ☐ = ☐

c. 5 + 5 + 5 + 5 ➡ ☐ × ☐ = ☐

Multiplication as Equal Distribution

3. Write a multiplication operation for each picture.

a.

☐ × ☐ = ☐

b.

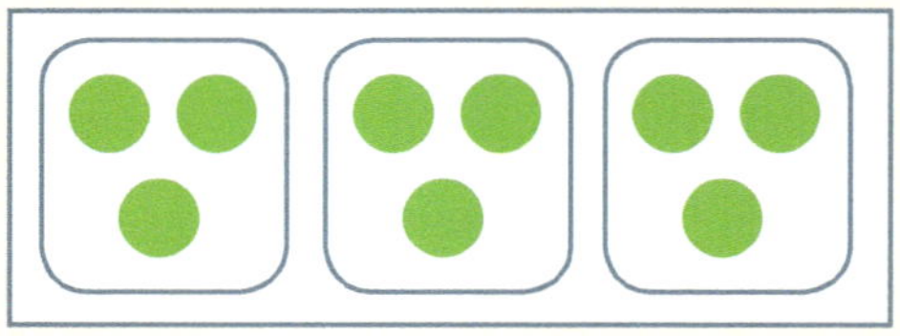

☐ × ☐ = ☐

Multiplication Using One Corresponding to Many

4. Represent the situations. Then, write the multiplication operations.

a. Isabella puts her toys in boxes. If she puts 10 toys in each box, how many toys will she put in 4 boxes?

1 box	2 boxes	3 boxes	4 boxes

☐ times ☐ is ☐

☐ × ☐ = ☐

b. Rachel put some fresh eggs in her refrigerator. If there are 2 rows with 8 eggs in each, how many eggs are there?

☐ times ☐ is ☐

☐ × ☐ = ☐

c. When you complete a level in a videogame, you earn 4 points. If Jane has passed 6 levels, how many points does she have?

1st level	2nd level	3rd level	4th level	5th level	6th level

☐ times ☐ is ☐

☐ × ☐ = ☐

How Did You Do?

For each ☺ color a ⬭.

Section 3

Multiplication Word Problems

Word Problems With Repeated Elements

Let's Connect

- What information do you need to answer the question? Write it.

____

____

- What operation can you use to answer the question? Write and solve it.

- What is the answer to the question? Write it.

____

Let's Learn

In math problems involving **repetition of elements**, you know the number of groups and the number of elements in each group. What you need to find out is the total number of elements, and you can find it using **multiplication**.

1. Identify the **important information** and the **question**. → 5 boxes with 10 pencils in each. How many pencils are there in total?
2. Choose a **strategy** to find the answer. → $5 \times 10 = 50$
3. **Answer** the question. → There are 50 pencils in total.

Let's Practice

1. Underline the important information and the question for each word problem. Then, solve them. Analyze

a. If Matt does 10 minutes of sit-ups a day, how many minutes of sit-ups does he do in a week?

You can represent each word problem with a picture. This makes them easier to solve.

Answer: ______________________________

b. To organize cups on a table, Marie puts them in 4 rows with 8 cups in each row. How many cups does Marie organize in total?

Answer: ______________________________

c. Camilla, Caroline and Lucy donated food to a retirement home. Each girl brought 4 loaves of bread, 3 kilograms of fruit and 10 yogurts. How many loaves of bread did the girls donate in total?

Answer: ______________________________

Exam Strategies

Look and Learn

Mark the correct answer with an ✕ .

Read the instructions carefully.

1 A doctor sees five children and five adults each day. How many patients does the doctor see, in total, in six days?

- A 10
- B 30
- ☒ C 60

Analyze each option. Mark the correct answer with an ✕ .

Read and understand the problem. Don't forget to identify the important information to find the answer.

In this case, you can add 5 + 5, first, to find the number of patients the doctor sees each day. Then, multiply that by 6 to find the answer to the problem.

Your Turn!

Mark the correct answer with an ✕ .

2 A bottle of juice is made of 150 ml of water and 50 ml of fruit pulp. How many mls do eight bottles of juice have in total?

- A 200 ml
- B 800 ml
- C 1,600 ml

What Did You Learn?

Final Evaluation

Counting by 3s, 4s and 5s

1. Count the elements by 4s and complete.

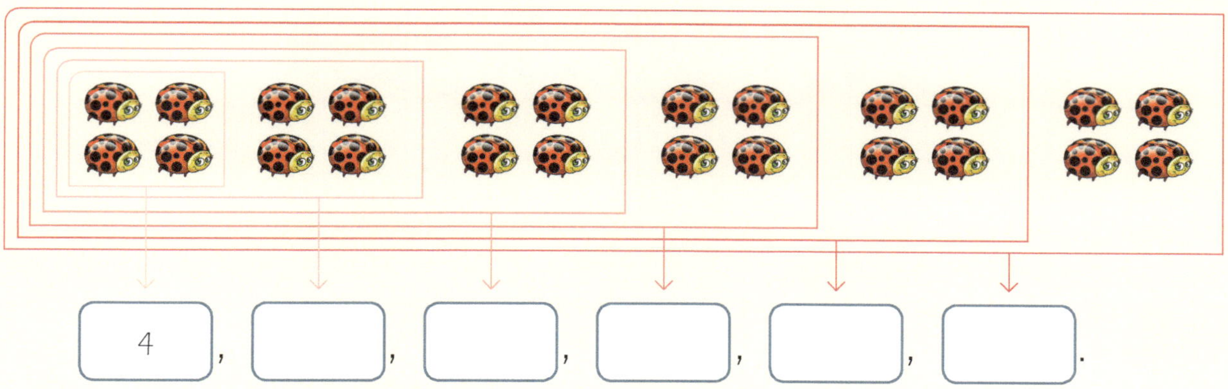

There are ________ groups of ________ .

There are ________ .

Relating Addition and Multiplication

2. Mark the operations that are correct with a ✔ and the ones that are incorrect with an ✖ .

a. ◯ $4 + 4 = 4 \times 4$

b. ◯ $3 + 3 + 3 + 3 = 4 \times 3$

c. ◯ $2 + 2 + 2 + 2 + 2 = 5 \times 2$

d. ◯ $6 + 6 + 6 + 6 + 6 + 6 = 6 \times 6$

Multiplication as Equal Distribution

3. Represent the situation with ●.

If Jack has seven bags with eight cookies in each, how many cookies does he have in total?

Multiplication Using One Corresponding to Many

4. Read the situation. Complete and answer.

For a family dinner, each person needs two glasses, three plates and five pieces of silverware. There are six people in the family.

a.

1 person	2 people	3 people	4 people	5 people	6 people

☐ glasses are needed.

b.

1 person	2 people	3 people	4 people	5 people	6 people

☐ plates are needed.

c.

1 person	2 people	3 people	4 people	5 people	6 people

☐ pieces of silverware are needed.

Word Problems With Repeated Elements

5. Solve the word problem.

A shoe maker fixes seven shoes a day. How many shoes will he fix from Monday to Saturday?

Answer: ______________________________

Mark the correct answer with an ✕ .

6. Anna has two $2,000 bills, three $500 coins and four $50 coins. How much money does Anna have?

A $2,550

B $5,700

C $6,750

7. Which operation is the answer to the problem?

Marcy has six cards on each of the nine pages of her album. How many cards does Marcy have?

A 9×6

B $9 + 6$

C $6 + 9$

8. Which operation is the answer to the problem?

If a baker sells ten cakes every day of the week, how many does he sell in total in a week?

A 10×5

B 10×7

C 20×7

Find Test 2 Study Page

How Did You Do?

For each color a .

Unit 3

Fractions and Location

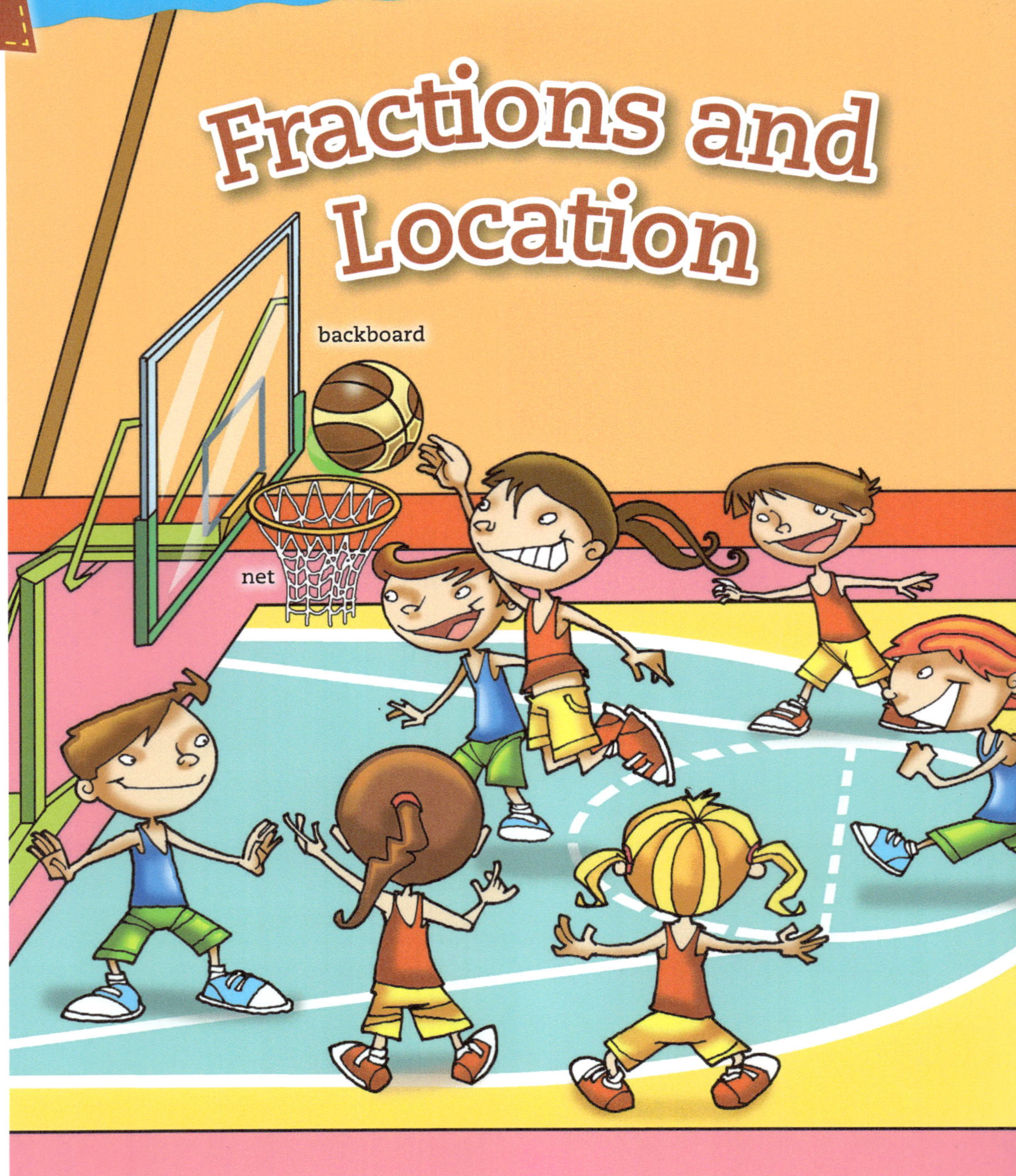

Key Words

whole

$\frac{4}{4}$ 

part

$\frac{1}{4}$ 

numerator

$\frac{1}{3}$

denominator

$\frac{1}{3}$

grid

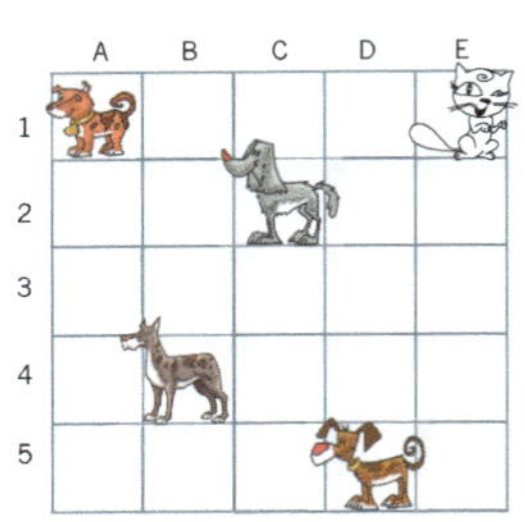

In this unit you will learn to:

- understand the concept of fractions.
- represent fractions as a whole and in parts.
- identify the terms of a fraction.
- describe the location of objects on maps and grids.
- understand translations on grids.
- work in an organized way.

What Do You Know? Initial Evaluation

Look at the picture and answer.

1. How many players does each team have?

   Each team has ☐ players.

2. Complete each sentence with the following words.

   twice   half

   a. The home team has scored ____________ as many points as the visiting team.

   b. The visiting team has scored ____________ the points scored by the home team.

3. How many quarters does a basketball game have? Circle your answer.

   1   2   3   4

4. Write the number of parts each color represents.

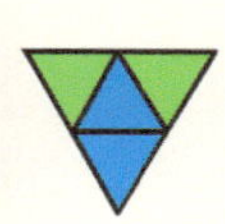

☐ parts of 4 parts

☐ parts of 4 parts

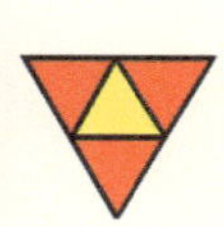

☐ parts of 4 parts

☐ part of 4 parts

The Concept of Part-Whole

Let's Connect

- How many cookies are there in the picture?

  There are ☐ cookies in total.

- How many cookies are the family eating in relation to the total number of cookies? Circle.

  1 out of 8 2 out of 8 3 out of 8 4 out of 8

- How many equal pieces of cheese are there?

  There are ☐ equal pieces.

- How many pieces of cheese are there on the plate? Circle.

  1 out of 4 2 out of 4 3 out of 4 4 out of 4

Education through Values

A nutritious and healthy breakfast including fruit, dairy products and grains will give you energy throughout the day!

Let's Learn

A **fraction** is a number that represents part of a whole or part of a group. In a fraction, each of the parts of the whole is always equal.

$\frac{2}{8}$ → 2: parts of the whole; 8: total number of parts the whole is divided into

- **Fraction** of a **whole**

$\frac{2}{8}$

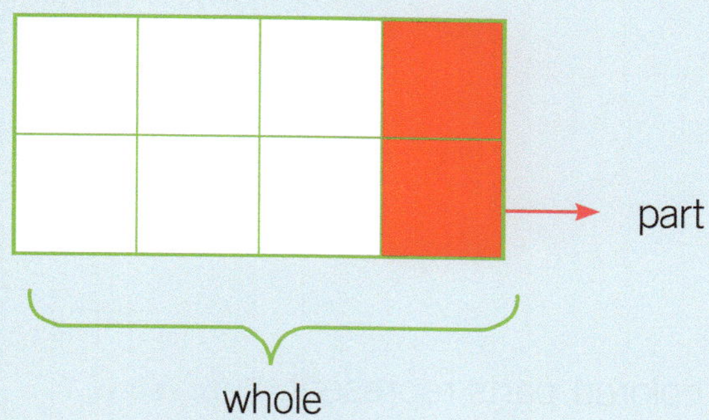

- **Fraction** of a **group of identical elements**

$\frac{2}{8}$

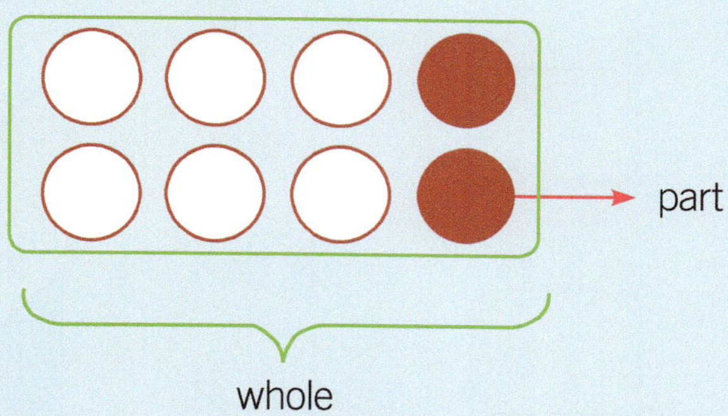

Whole fractions have the same number above and below the fraction bar, for example, $\frac{1}{1}$, $\frac{2}{2}$, $\frac{12}{12}$, etc.

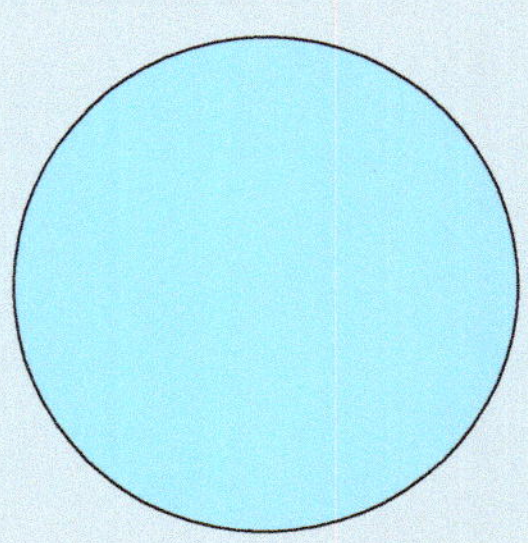

$\frac{1}{1}$

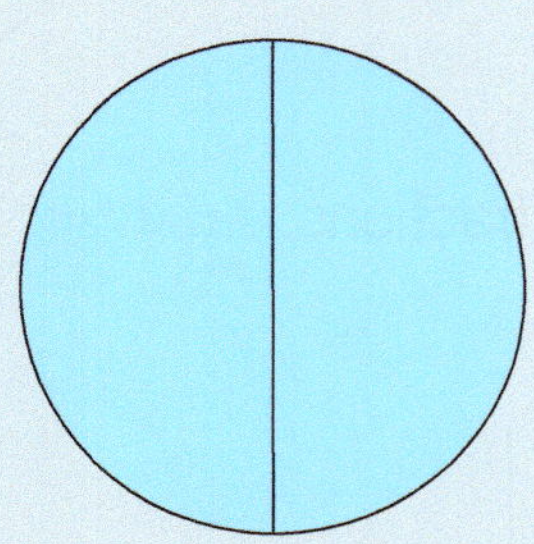

$\frac{2}{2}$

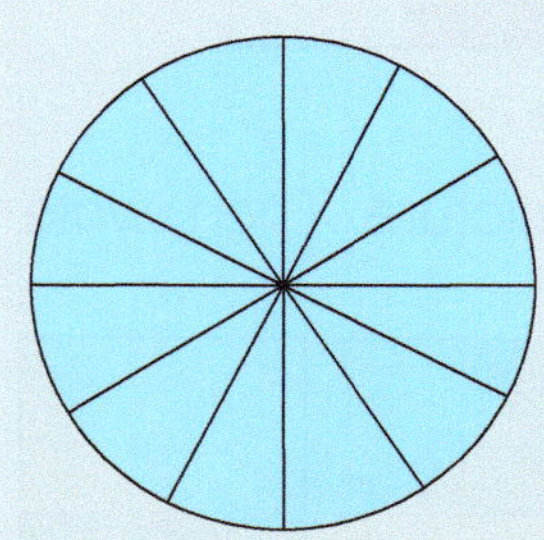

$\frac{12}{12}$

Let's Practice

1. Color the fractions. Represent

a. $\frac{1}{2}$

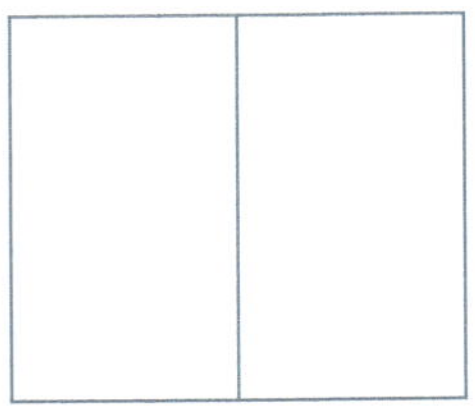

b. $\frac{2}{3}$

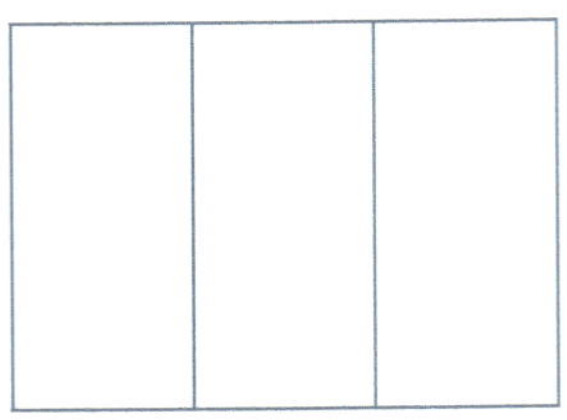

c. $\frac{1}{4}$

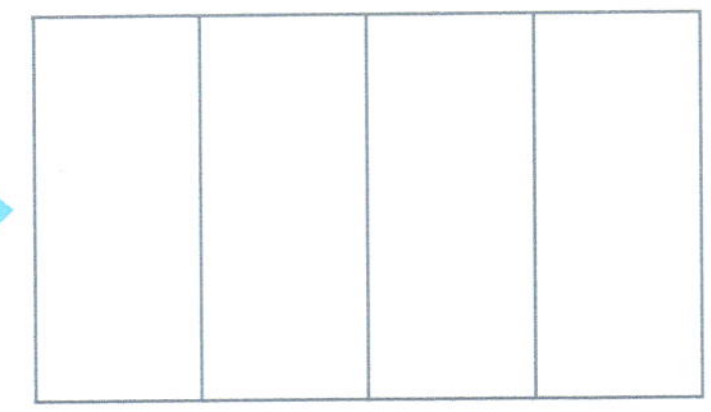

d. $\frac{3}{5}$

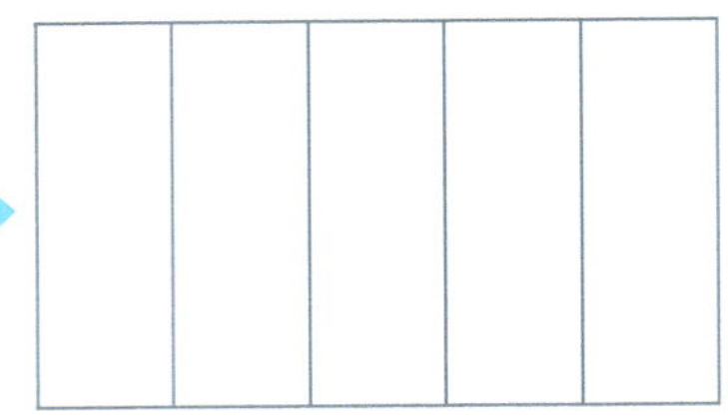

2. Write the fractions that the colored parts represent. Represent

a.

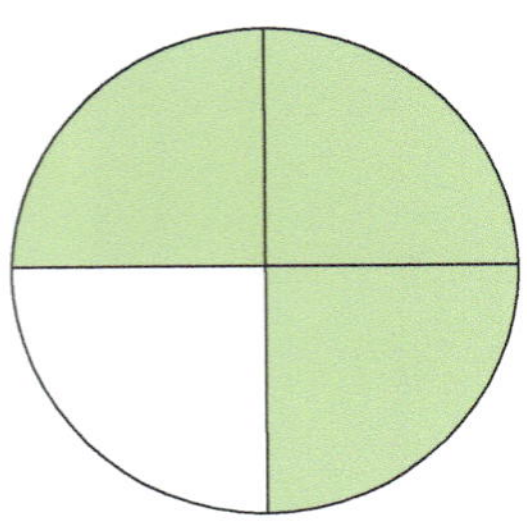

b.

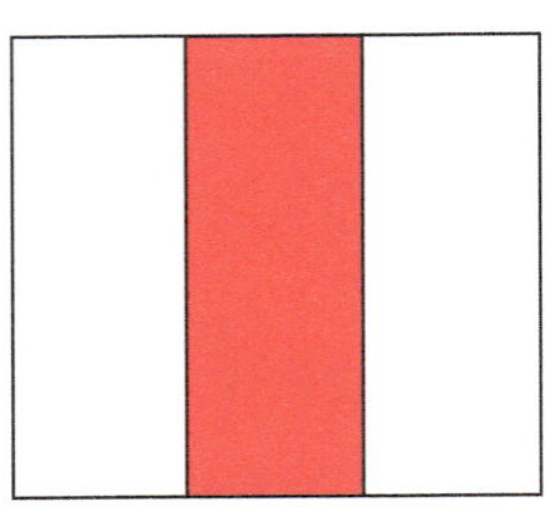

c.

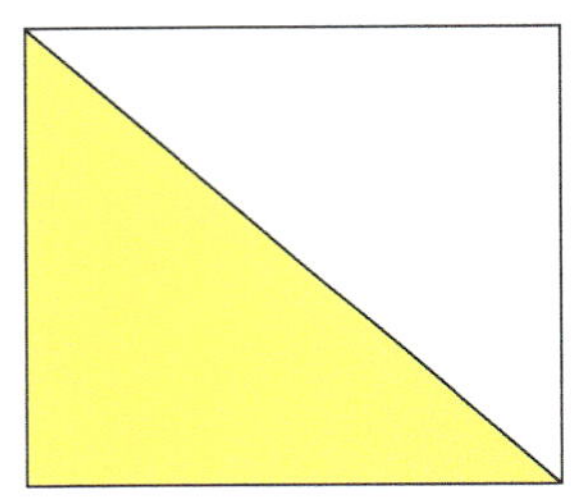

d.

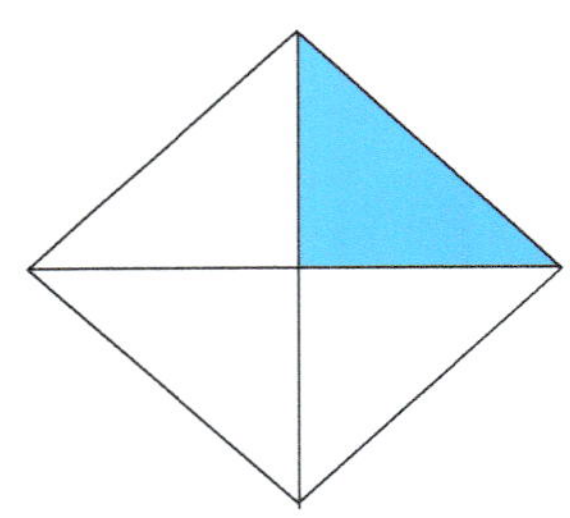

3. Look at the picture. Then, write the correct fractions. Analyze

parts

parts

4. Color the circles to represent the fractions. Represent

a. $\frac{5}{6}$ ▶

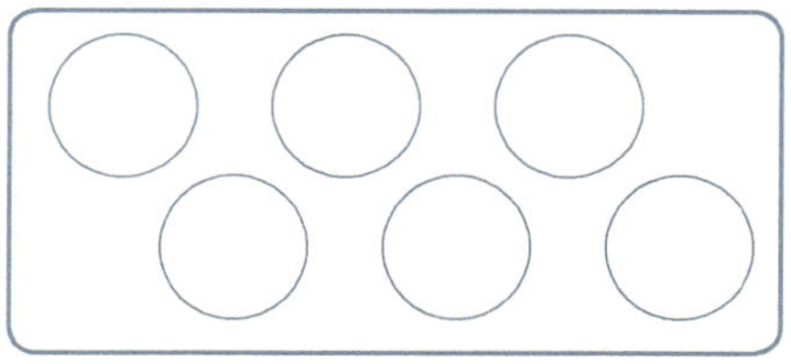

c. $\frac{2}{5}$ ▶

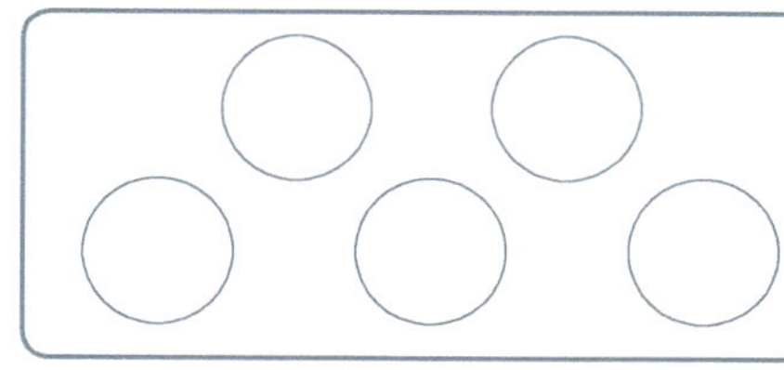

b. $\frac{1}{3}$ ▶

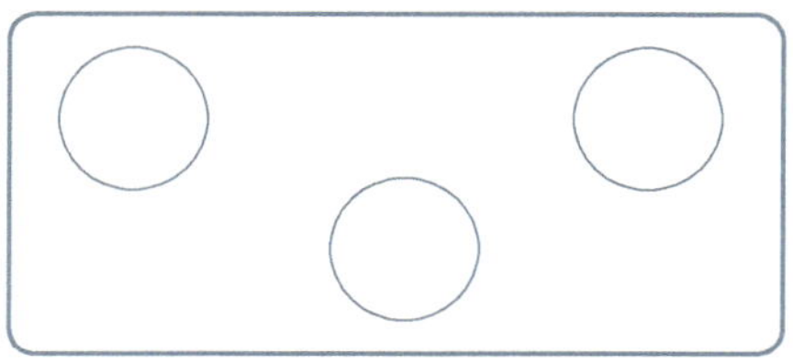

d. $\frac{3}{4}$ ▶

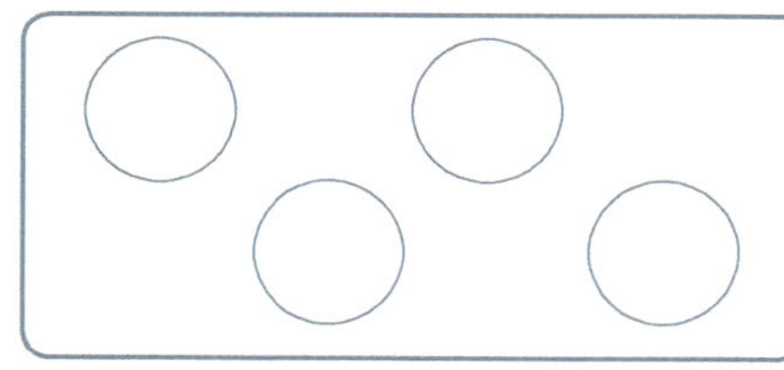

5. Write the fractions that the colored parts represent. Represent

a.

▶ ____

c.

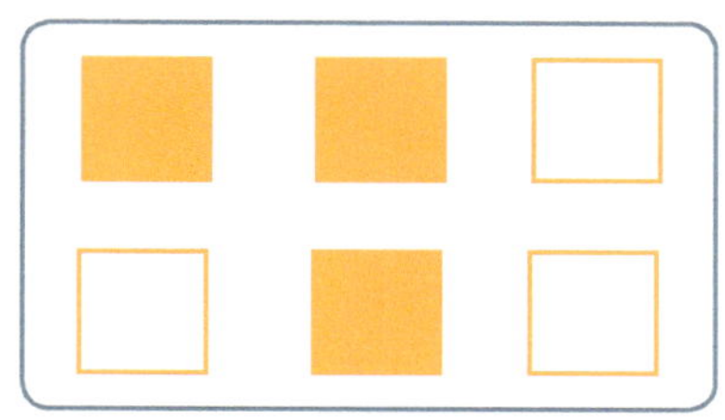

▶ ____

b.

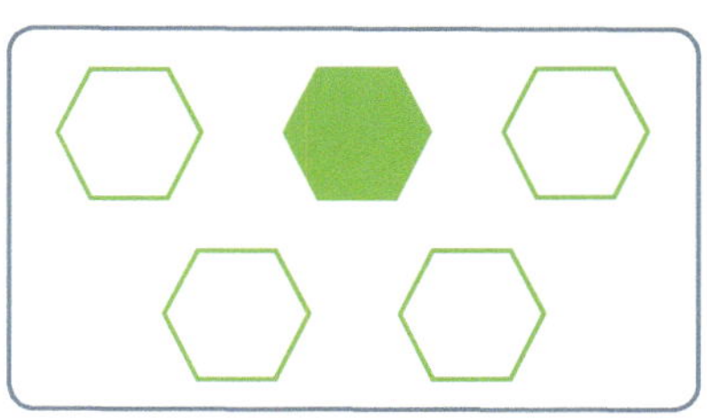

▶ ____

d.

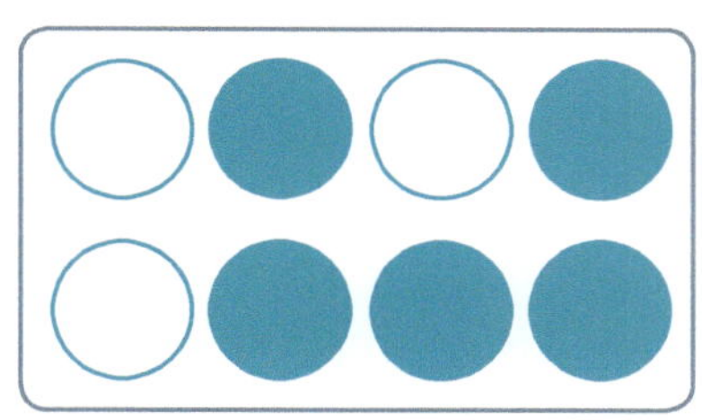

▶ ____

6. Look at the group of elements. Then, write the fractions. Analyze

____ ▶ parts

____ ▶ parts

Terms of a Fraction

Let's Connect

- How many equal slices was the pizza divided into?

It was divided into ☐ equal slices.

- How many slices of pizza are on the table.

There are ☐ slices of pizza on the table.

- What fraction represents the part of the pizza on the table?

$\frac{\square}{\square}$
→ parts of the whole
→ total number of parts

Let's Learn

The **terms of a fraction** are:

$\frac{1}{4}$
→ **Numerator**: parts of the whole
→ **Fraction bar**: line that separates the numerator from the denominator
→ **Denominator**: parts the whole is divided into

Let's Practice

1. Complete the table. Interpret

	Representation	Numerator	Denominator	Fraction
a.	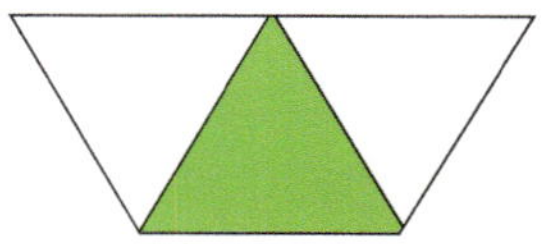			
b.	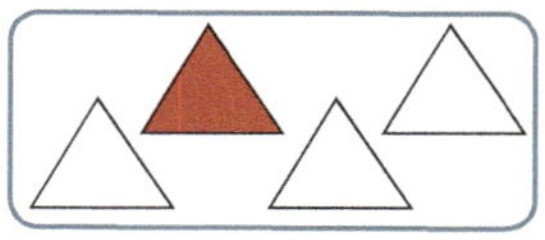			
c.	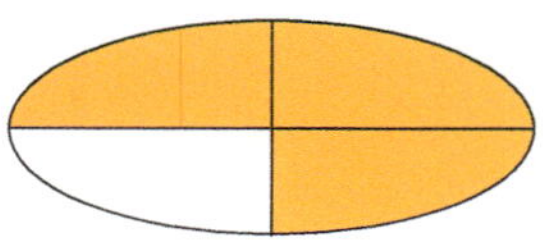			

2. Match each description to a fraction. Analyze

The denominator is more than double the numerator.

The numerator is half the denominator.

$\frac{2}{5}$

$\frac{4}{6}$

$\frac{1}{2}$

Challenge

Pizza Time! Use construction paper to make your own pizza. Put different toppings on different parts of your pizza. Use fractions to describe your pizza.

3. Read the problems and solve them. Analyze

a. My numerator is twice the number 3, and my denominator is twice my numerator. What fraction am I?

b. My denominator is 5 more than my numerator. My numerator is the number of days in a week. What fraction am I?

Reading Fractions

Let's Connect

Fruit Salad

(4 servings)

- 6 apples
- 4 strawberries
- $\frac{1}{2}$ banana
- $\frac{1}{4}$ melon
- $\frac{3}{4}$ cup of orange juice

- How much fruit do you need to make a fruit salad? Write each amount in word form.

Apples: ______________________ Strawberries: ______________________

- How do you read the amount of melon in the fruit salad? Write it in word form.

Melon: ______________________

Remember!

We say *one half*, but *two halves*.

Let's Learn

To **read a fraction**, read its terms like this:

First, read the **numerator**.

Second, read the **denominator** as an ordinal number.

Denominator	2	3	4	5	6	7	8	9
Read as	half	third	fourth	fifth	sixth	seventh	eighth	ninth

For example:

$\frac{1}{2}$ is read as **one-half**. $\frac{3}{4}$ is read as **three-fourths**. $\frac{5}{7}$ is read as **five-sevenths**.

Let's Practice

1. Write each fraction in word form. Represent

a. $\frac{3}{5}$ ▶ ____________________

c. $\frac{1}{4}$ ▶ ____________________

b. $\frac{2}{3}$ ▶ ____________________

d. $\frac{4}{6}$ ▶ ____________________

2. Write the fractions. Represent

a. four-fifths ▶ $\frac{\square}{\square}$

c. one-seventh ▶ $\frac{\square}{\square}$

b. three-ninths ▶ $\frac{\square}{\square}$

d. two-eighths ▶ $\frac{\square}{\square}$

3. Complete the table. Interpret

	Representation	Fraction	Word Form
a.	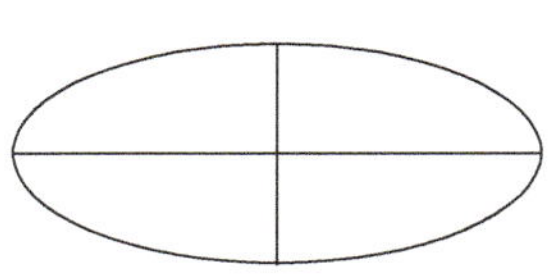	$\frac{1}{4}$	____________________
b.	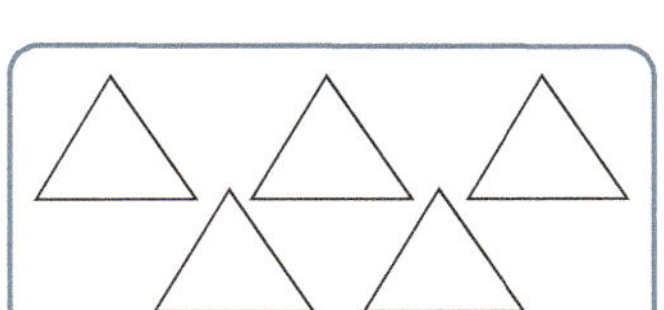	$\frac{\square}{\square}$	two-fifths
c.	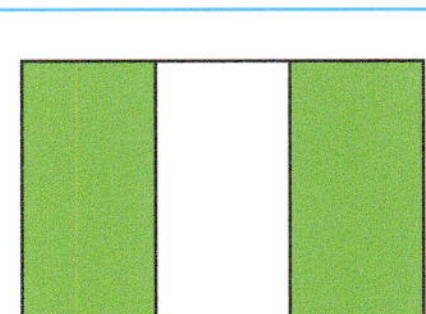	$\frac{\square}{\square}$	____________________

Basic Fractions

Let's Connect

- How many equal parts was the cake divided into?

It was divided into ☐ equal parts.

- Someone eats a piece of cake. What fraction of the whole does that piece represent? Write it in numbers and in word form.

$\frac{\square}{\square}$ ▸ ______________________

Let's Learn

Halves, **thirds** and **fourths** are often used in daily life.

To make...

- halves,... divide into two equal parts.

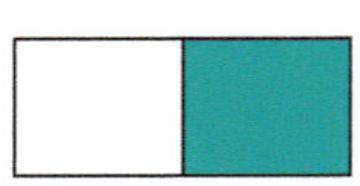

$\frac{1}{2}$ one-half

One part out of two parts is colored.

- thirds,... divide into three equal parts.

$\frac{1}{3}$ one-third

One part out of three parts is colored.

- fourths,... divide into four equal parts.

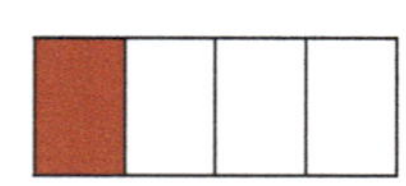

$\frac{1}{4}$ one-fourth

One part out of four parts is colored.

Let's Practice

1. Read the fractions and divide the pizzas. Then, color the parts to represent the fractions. Represent

a. $\frac{1}{2}$ **b.** $\frac{1}{4}$ **c.** $\frac{3}{6}$

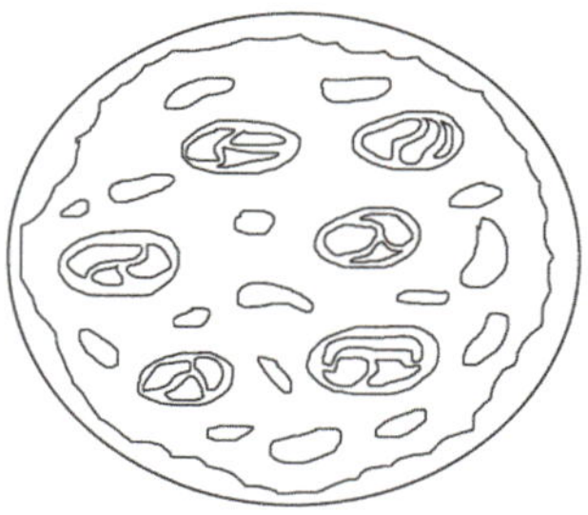

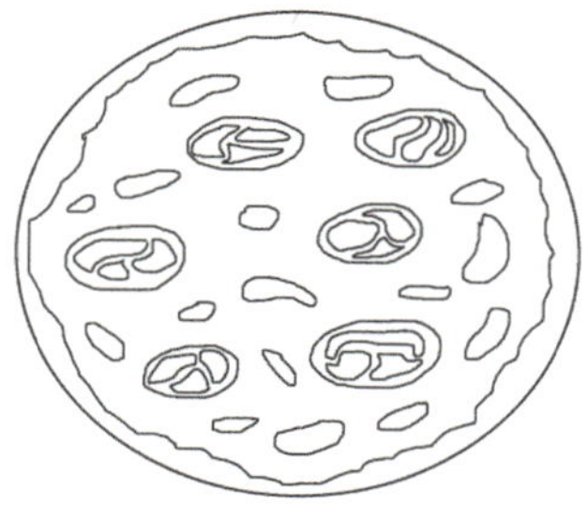

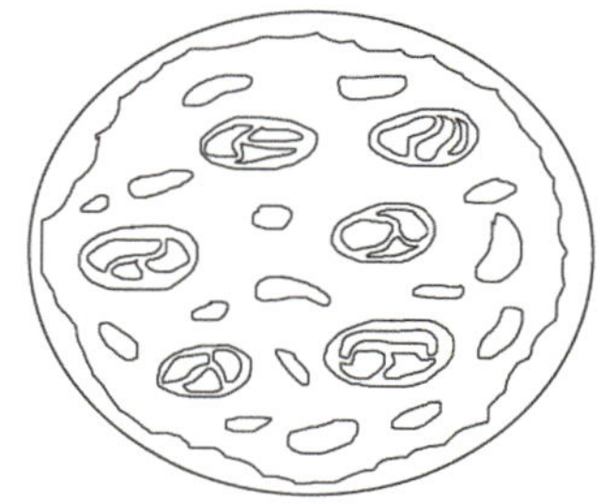

2. Color the rectangles to represent the fractions. Represent

a. $\frac{2}{3}$

b. $\frac{1}{3}$

c. $\frac{2}{4}$

d. $\frac{3}{5}$

Quiz Yourself

Look at the shape and answer.

- What fraction corresponds to the parts?

▶ parts

- Which other colors, together, represent the same fraction? Write the colors and the fraction.

Colors: ______________________ Fraction ▶

Let's Check!

The Concept of Part-Whole

1. Represent the fractions.

a. $\frac{2}{3}$

b. $\frac{4}{5}$

Terms of a Fraction

2. Look at the picture and complete.

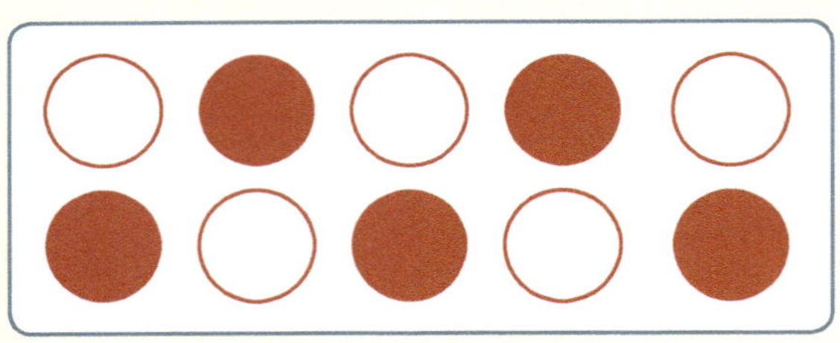

a. There are ______ circles in total.

b. There are ______ red circles.

c. The fraction represented by the picture has a numerator of ______ and a denominator of ______.

Reading Fractions

3. Write fractions in word form.

a.

▸ ______________________

b.

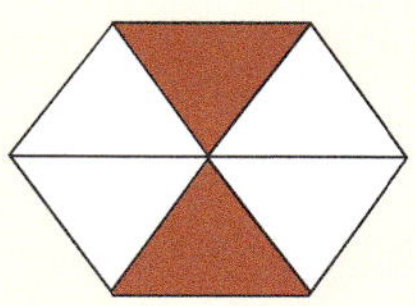

▸ ______________________

c.

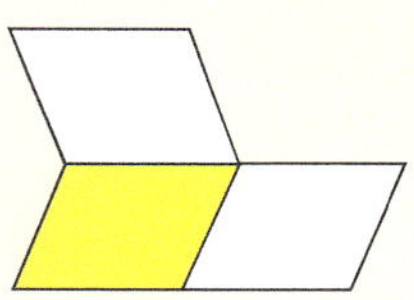

▸ ______________________

4. Write the fractions in numbers.

a. four-sixths

b. three-fourths

c. two-thirds

How Did You Do?

For each 🐸 color a ⬭.

Location on a Map

Let's Connect

Springwood School

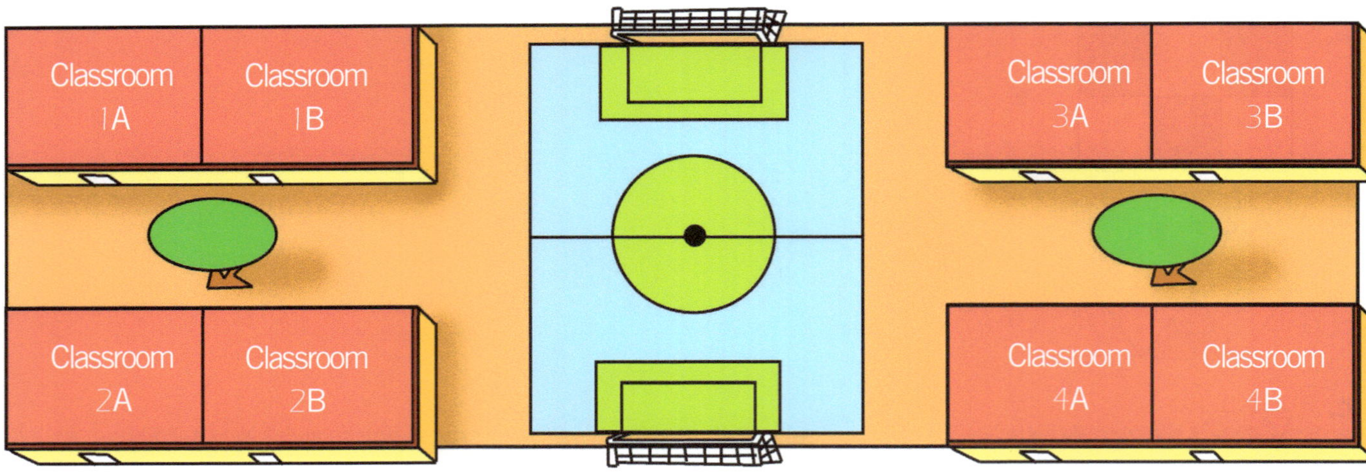

- Circle the classrooms on the left side of the map.
- Which classroom is to the right of 3A?

  ____

- Where is classroom 2B located? Describe its location.

  ____

  ____

Let's Learn

To describe the location of something on a map, you can use different **points of reference** and **positions**. For example, *above, below, to the left* or *to the right*.

Let's Practice

1. Look at the map. Describe the location of the places mentioned in relation to other places and streets on the map. Apply

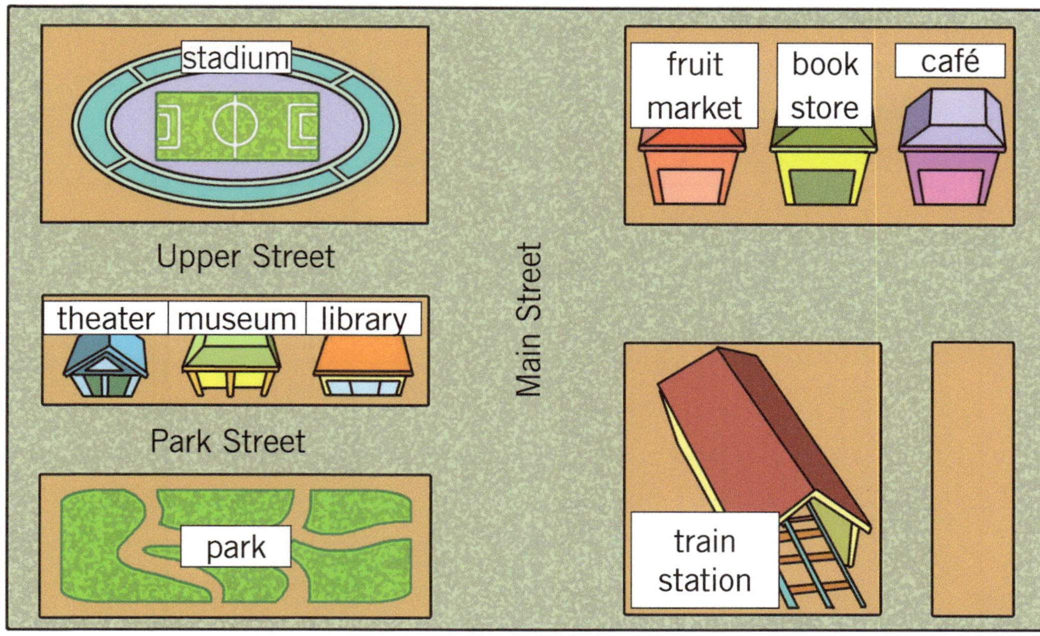

a. The book store is located ______________________________

____

____

b. The train station is located ______________________________

____

____

c. The museum is located ______________________________

____

____

Did You Know...?

Your sense of direction is your ability to know your location and find where things are located.

Location on a Grid

Let's Connect

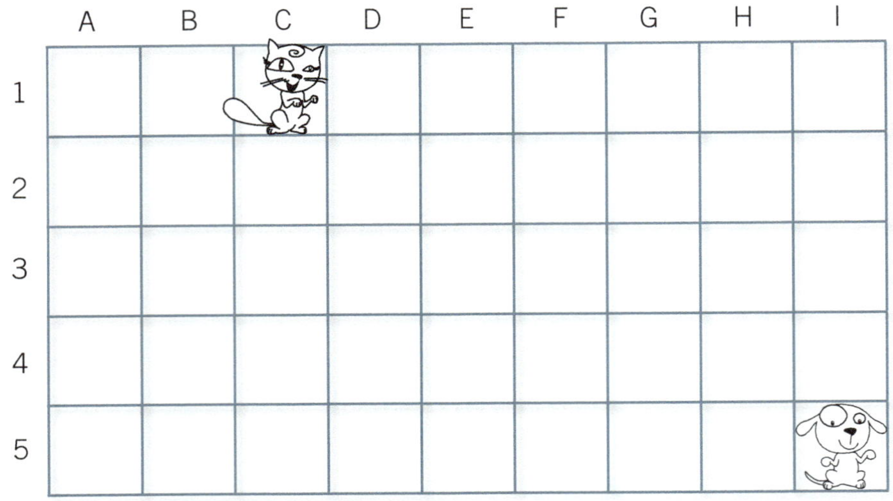

- How does  get to the same square as ? Check the correct answer.

  ◯ He moves 4 squares up and 6 to the left.

  ◯ He moves 4 squares up and 6 to the right.

Tip

Coordinates are a set of numbers or values that represent the exact position of something.

- Describe the location of  using the letters and numbers on the grid.

____

____

Let's Learn

To describe the location of something on a grid, identify a **point of reference** and count the **squares** between the different **positions**. You can also use **coordinates** which are represented by letters and numbers. For example:

 is located **4 squares up** and **6 squares to the left** of . → point of reference

 is located in square C1.

Let's Practice

1. Look at the grid and describe the location of each dog. For **a** and **b** use  as a point of reference. For **c** and **d** write the coordinates. Apply

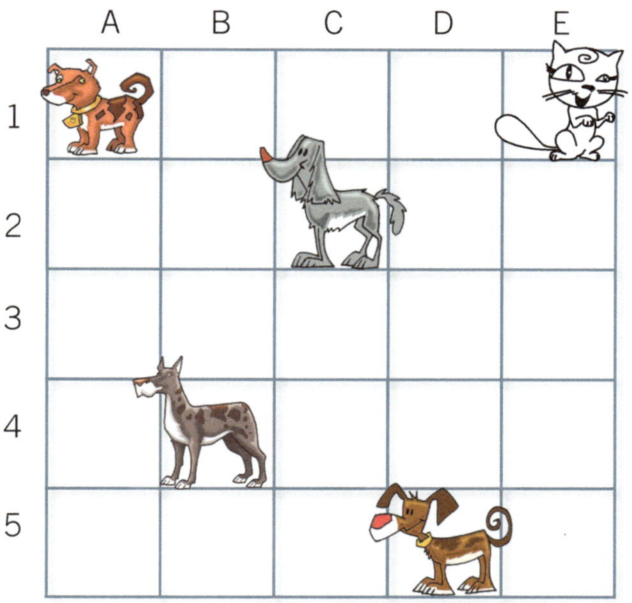

a.  is located ______________________________

______________________________ .

b.  is located ______________________________

______________________________ .

c.  is located ______________________________.

d.  is located ______________________________.

Quiz Yourself

Look at the grid. Use the descriptions of the locations of the objects to find them. Write their names.

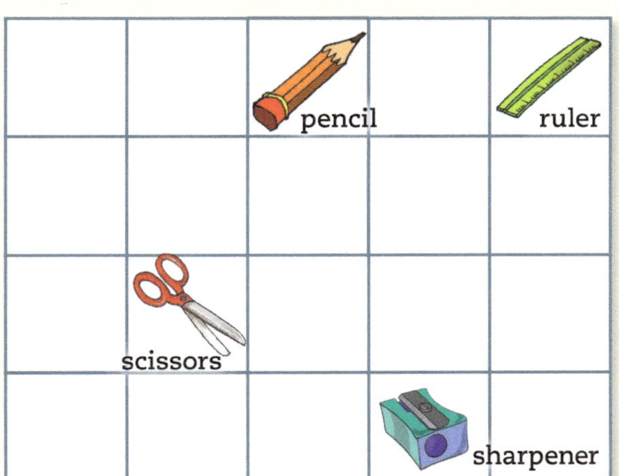

- It is located three squares below and one square to the right of the .

  ____

- It is located two squares above and three squares to the right of the 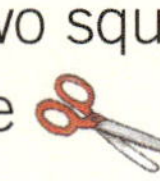.

  ____

- It is located three squares above and one square to the left of the .

  ____

Translation on a Grid

Let's Connect

Grid 1

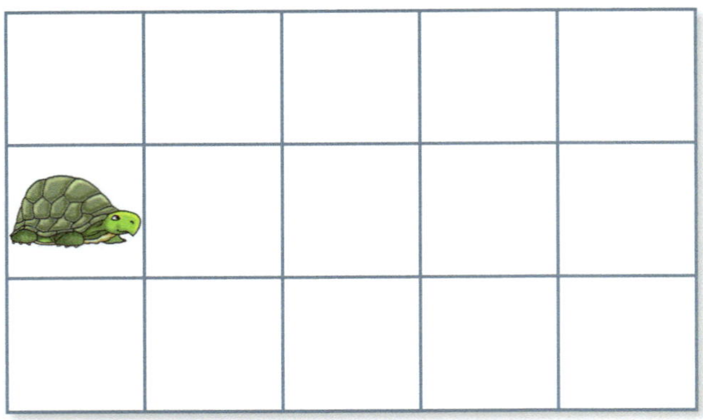

Grid 2

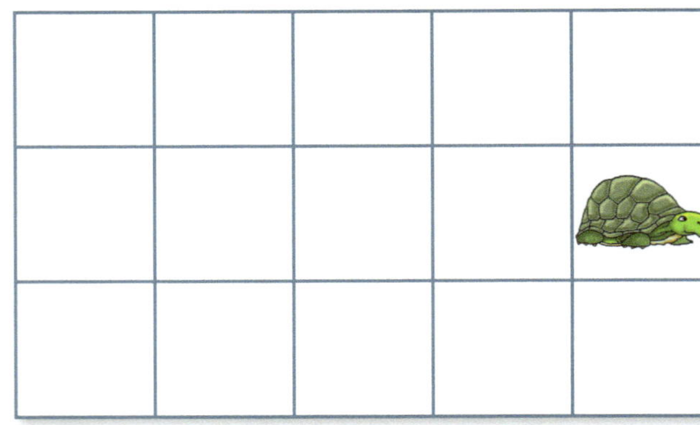

- What is the difference between the turtles in grids 1 and 2? Trace the answer.

size shape location

- What is the location of the turtle in **Grid 2** with respect to the one in **Grid 1**? Check the correct answer.

◯ 4 squares to the right.

◯ 4 squares to the left.

Let's Learn

A **translation** is movement in a straight line in any direction. This changes its location on a map or grid, but it doesn't change its shape, size or orientation.

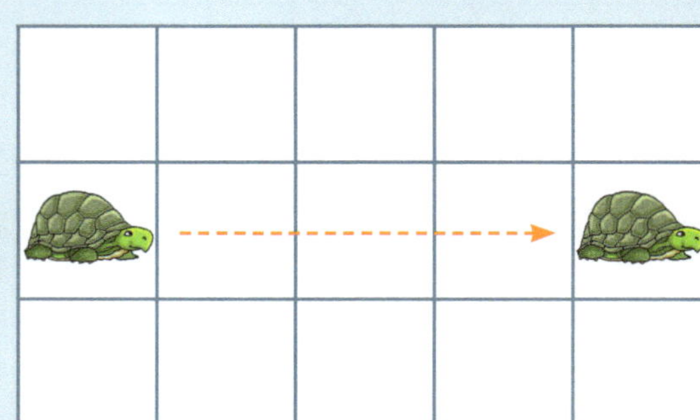

Let's Practice

1. Look at the red arrows. Then, color the translated arrows. Recognize

a.

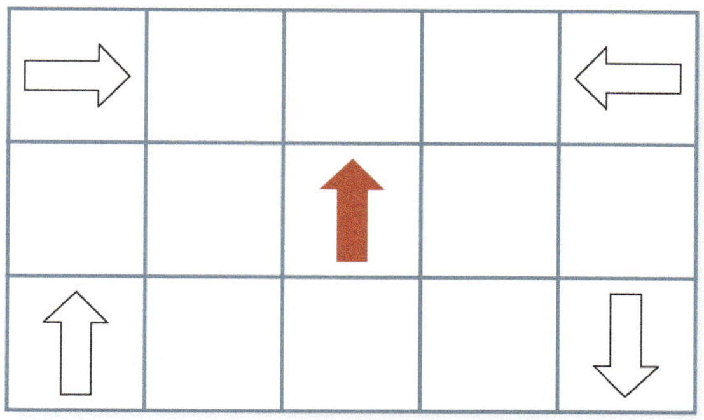

b.

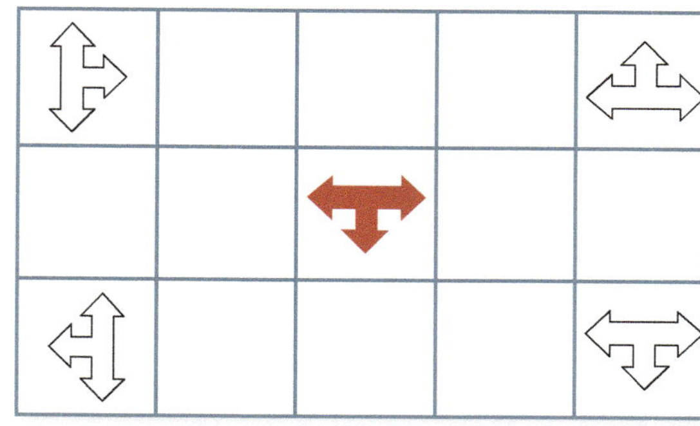

2. Color the dogs that were translated from . Recognize

Challenge

Act out activity two with your friends! One person will be the point of reference. Call out directions like, *"Take 2 steps back and 1 step left."* If somebody gets an instruction wrong, they miss a turn!

3. Translate each arrow according to the instructions. Apply

a. 4 squares to the right and 1 up.

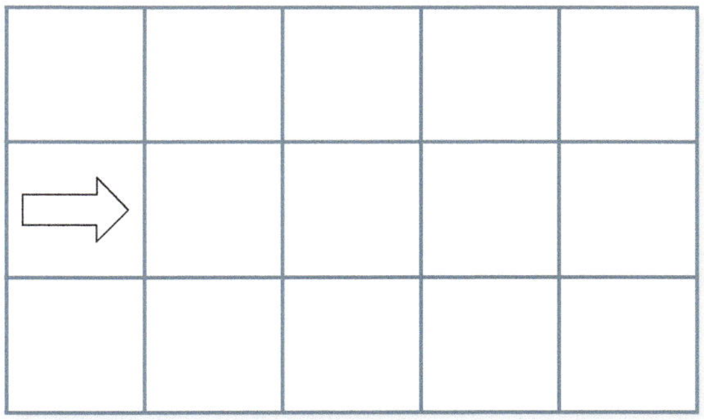

b. 2 squares up and 1 to the left.

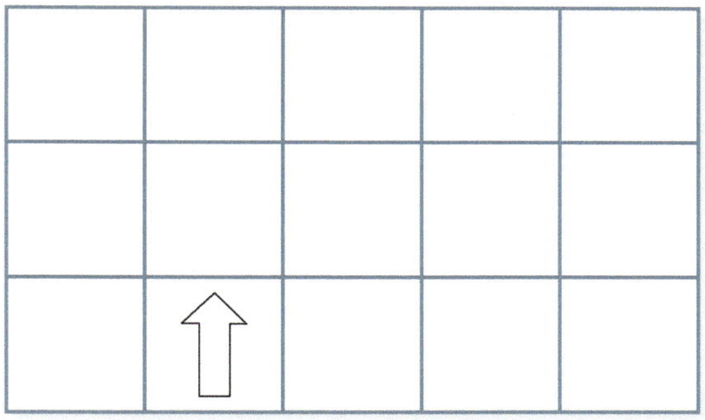

Exam Strategies

Look and Learn

Mark the correct answer with an ✗.

Read the instructions carefully.

1 Frank divided a piece of paper into 8 equal parts and then used $\frac{5}{8}$ of them. What portion of the paper did he not use?

A $\frac{5}{8}$

☒ B $\frac{3}{8}$

C $\frac{8}{8}$

D $\frac{3}{5}$

Read and understand the problem. Use a strategy that helps you add and subtract parts of a whole to find the answer.

Find the correct answer and mark it with an ✗.

Your Turn!

Mark the correct answer with an ✗.

2 Isabella divided her garden into 6 equal sections. If she grew lettuce in $\frac{2}{6}$ of her garden, what section of the garden is available to grow other vegetables?

A $\frac{3}{6}$

B $\frac{2}{6}$

C $\frac{2}{4}$

D $\frac{4}{6}$

What Did You Learn?

Final Evaluation

The Concept of Part-Whole

1. Color and represent each fraction.

a. $\frac{1}{2}$ 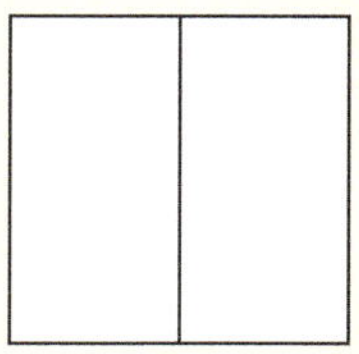

b. $\frac{2}{3}$ 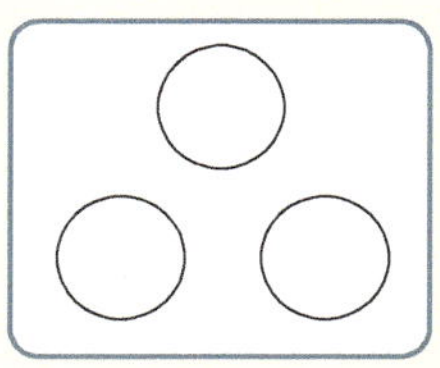

c. $\frac{1}{4}$ 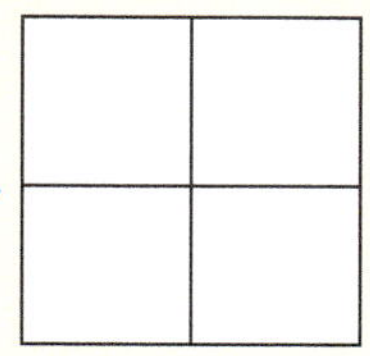

d. $\frac{3}{4}$ 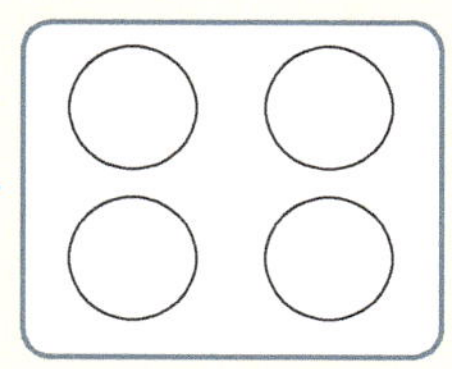

Terms of a Fraction

2. Complete the table.

	Fraction	Numerator	Denominator
a.	$\frac{1}{3}$		
b.	$\frac{2}{5}$		

Reading Fractions

3. Write the representations of fractions in word form.

a. 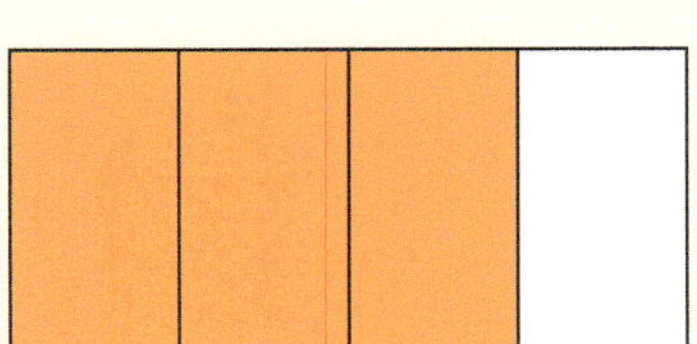

____

b. 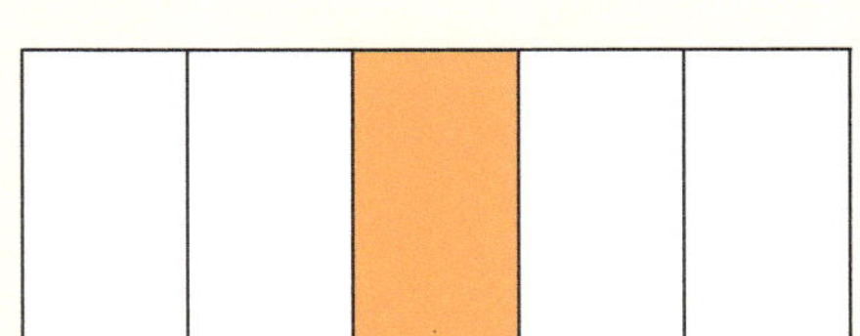

____

Location on a Map

4. Look at the map. Write the names of the places described.

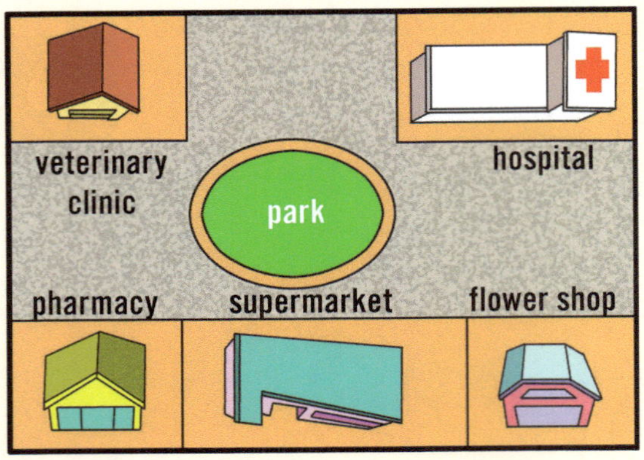

a. It is to the right of the pharmacy and to the left of the flower shop.

____

b. It is to the right of the park and above the flower shop.

____

Location on a Grid

5. Write which animal's location is described.

a. It is two squares to the right and one above the ▲.

____

b. It is three squares to the right and one below the ▲.

____

Translation on a Grid

6. Look at the red arrow. Then color the translated arrows.

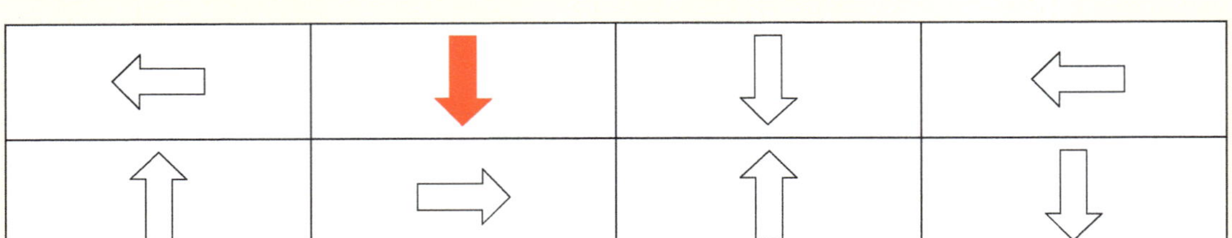

Mark the correct answer with an ✕.

7. Which fraction do the parts represent?

A $\frac{4}{8}$ **B** $\frac{2}{8}$ **C** $\frac{3}{8}$ **D** $\frac{1}{4}$

Use the grid to answer questions 8 and 9.

8. Which square is located in?

A A4

B B1

C D3

D F1

---

9. Which square is located in?

A A4

B B1

C D3

D F1

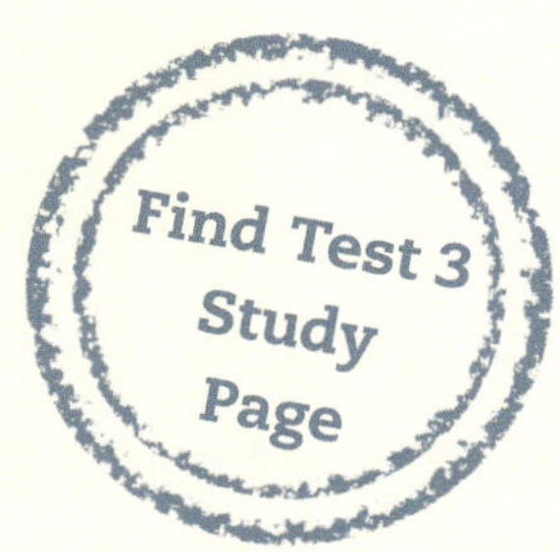

How Did You Do?

For each color a .

Unit 4

Numbers and Time

Key Words

place value chart

Th	H	T	O
4	5	6	9

number line

timeline

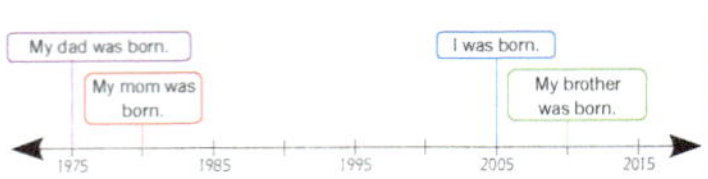

calendar

August						
M	T	W	T	F	S	S
			1	2	3	4
5	6	7	8	9	10	11
12	13	14	15	16	17	18
19	20	21	22	23	24	25
26	27	28	29	30	31	

In this unit you will learn to:

- read, write and represent numbers up to 100,000.
- represent numbers based on the place value of their digits.
- compose and decompose numbers, and put them in order.
- round numbers.
- read and interpret calendars and timelines.
- read and record time on digital and analog clocks.
- do your work in a clear and organized way.

What Do You Know? Initial Evaluation

Look at the picture and answer.

1. How many people are visiting the museum?

2. Round the number of people at the museum to the nearest ten.

3. How much do tickets for senior citizens cost? Write the price in word form.

4. What time does the museum close?

5. Write the years for the monuments on the timeline.

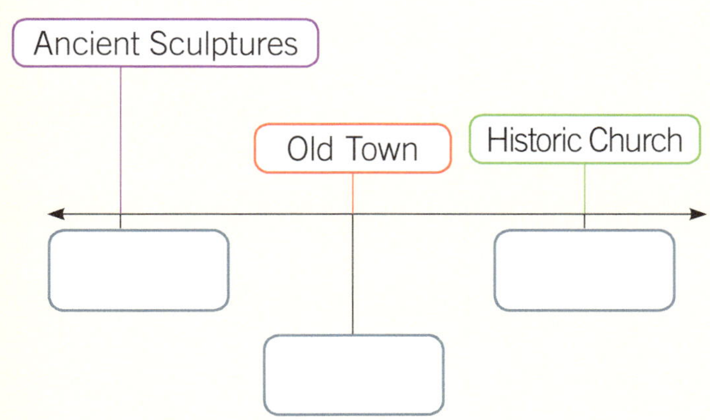

Thousands and Ten Thousands

Let's Connect

- How many digits does Mike's number have?

  It has ☐ digits.

- What number is Mike thinking of?

  ☐

- How many ones do six thousands equal?

  Six thousands equal ☐ ones.

Remember!

Place a comma between the thousands and the hundreds.

Tip

Equivalent means equal to and is represented by an = sign.

Let's Learn

The position of a digit in a number is its place value. The thousands place value and the ten thousands place value can be written **Th** and **TTh**.

Ten Thousands	Thousands	Hundreds	Tens	Ones
TTh	**Th**	**H**	**T**	**O**
1	0	0	0	0

	1 **Th** =	10 **H**	100 **T**	1,000 **O**

1 **TTh** =	10 **Th**	100 **H**	1,000 **T**	10,000 **O**

Let's Practice

1. Use the key to complete the representations of the numbers. Represent

■ = 1 O  = 1 T  = 1 H 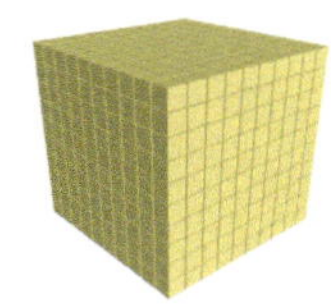 = 1 Th

a. 1 Th

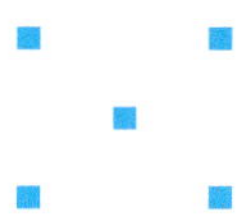

b. 1 TTh

2. Complete the equivalences. Interpret

a. 5 TTh equal ______ O.

b. 7 Th equal ______ O.

c. 4,000 O equal ______ Th.

d. 80,000 O equal ______ TTh.

3. Complete the equivalences with TTh, Th, H, T or O. Interpret

a. 6 TTh equal 60,000 ______.

b. 3 Th equal 3,000 ______.

c. 8,000 O equal 8 ______.

d. 90,000 O equal 9 ______.

Place Value

Let's Connect

- What number can Lucy represent with all the money?

[ ]

- Write the place value of the number.

Th	H	T	O

- If you switch the digit in the thousands place and the digit in the tens place, what number do you have?

[ ]

Word Focus

To **switch** means to change places.

Let's Learn

Each digit of a number has a **value** depending on its **position**. The **place value** of a digit is defined by the number of ones it has.

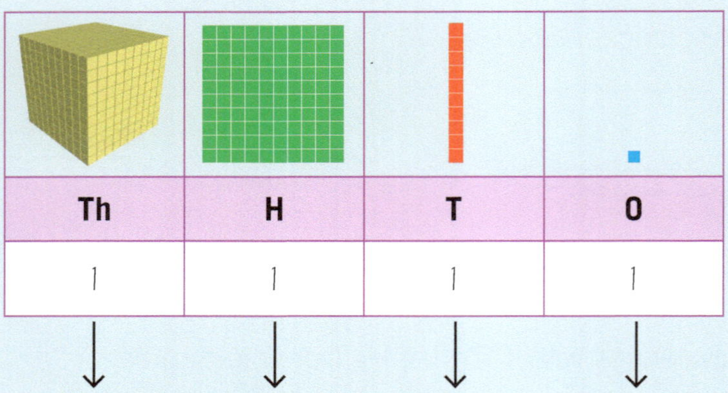

Th	H	T	O	
Th	**H**	**T**	**O**	name of place
1	1	1	1	number
↓ 1,000 ones	↓ 100 ones	↓ 10 ones	↓ 1 ones	place value

Let's Practice

1. Complete the table with the place name and place value of the digit in red in each number. Understand

	Number	Place Name	Place Value
a.	2,056		
b.	5,302		
c.	8,695		
d.	6,741		
e.	9,357		

2. Write three numbers that fit each description. Exemplify

a. Numbers where 4 has a place value of 4,000 ones.

b. Numbers where 7 has a place value of 700 ones.

c. Numbers where 9 has a place value of 90 ones.

3. Look at the numbers and answer. Analyze

4,301	638	7,923

a. Which digit is repeated in all of the numbers? Circle it.

b. In which number does the repeated digit have a place value of 300 ones? Write the number in word form.

Composing and Decomposing Numbers

Let's Connect

- How many thousands does the number Ben represented have? ☐ Th
- What is the place value of the digit located in the hundreds place in Ben's number? ☐
- What number did Ben represent? ☐

Let's Learn

Numbers can be **decomposed** and **composed** using **addition**.

- **Decomposition:**

using the **names** of the places	using the place **values** of the digits
2,345 = 2 **Th** + 3 **H** + 4 **T** + 5 **O**	2,345 = 2,000 + 300 + 40 + 5

- **Composition:**

using the **names** of the places	using the place **values** of the digits
2 **Th** + 3 **H** + 4 **T** + 5 **O** = 2,345	2,000 + 300 + 40 + 5 = 2,345

Let's Practice

1. Decompose the numbers according to the place values of their digits. Apply

a. 1,342 = ☐ + ☐ + ☐ + ☐

b. 2,539 = ☐ + ☐ + ☐ + ☐

c. 3,472 = ☐ + ☐ + ☐ + ☐

d. 7,144 = ☐ + ☐ + ☐ + ☐

e. 9,183 = ☐ + ☐ + ☐ + ☐

2. Compose the numbers. Apply

a. 3,000 + 600 + 50 + 9 = ☐

b. 6 Th + 4 H + 7 T + 8 O = ☐

c. 7,000 + 200 + 60 + 3 = ☐

d. 5 Th + 8 H + 4 O = ☐

e. 9,000 + 30 + 5 = ☐

f. 8 Th + 9 H + 1 T = ☐

Quiz Yourself

Read the problem and answer.

Each digit of a number is written according to its place or place value.

60

3 Th

1

9 H

- What is the number? Write the number in the box and then write it in word form.

☐ ➡ ______________________________

Let's Check!

Thousands and Ten Thousands

1. Circle the ten thousands and complete the equivalence.

_____ Th = _____ TTh

2. Circle the equivalent expressions.

a.	5 TTh ➡	50,000 O	50,000 T	50,000 H
b.	7 Th ➡	7,000 T	7,000 O	7,000 H
c.	3 Th ➡	3,000 T	3,000 H	3,000 O
d.	6 TTh ➡	60,000 T	60,000 H	60,000 O

Place Value

3. Color the numbers described.

a. The digit in the hundreds place has a value of 500 ones.

5,459	5,545	55,125	51,515

b. The digit in the ten thousands place has a value of 40,000 ones.

41,000	4,444	34,444	40,000

c. The digit in the thousands place has a value of 7,000 ones.

7,777	71,000	70,000	7,257

d. The digit in the tens place has a value of 90 ones.

9,909	9,090	909	91,991

Composing and Decomposing Numbers

4. Decompose each number and write the names of the places, above, and the place values of the digits below.

a. 3,542 =

b. 7,964 =

c. 9,815 =

d. 5,101 =

How Did You Do?

For each (frog) color a (lily pad).

Section 2
Order and Comparison of Numbers

Comparing Numbers Using a Place Value Chart

Let's Connect

- How many Th, H, T and O does each girl have?

Th	H	T	O

Th	H	T	O

- Who has more money? Circle.

Let's Learn

You can use a **place value chart** to **compare** numbers. Compare, from left to right, the digits in the **same position** for each number.

Th	H	T	O
4	5	7	9

Th	H	T	O
4	5	6	9

4 **Th** = 4 **Th**

5 **H** = 5 **H**

7 **T** > 6 **T**

So, 4,579 is **greater than** 4,569.

4,579 > 4,569

Let's Practice

1. Answer using the place value chart. Apply

a. Which number is greater, 3,947 or 3,949?

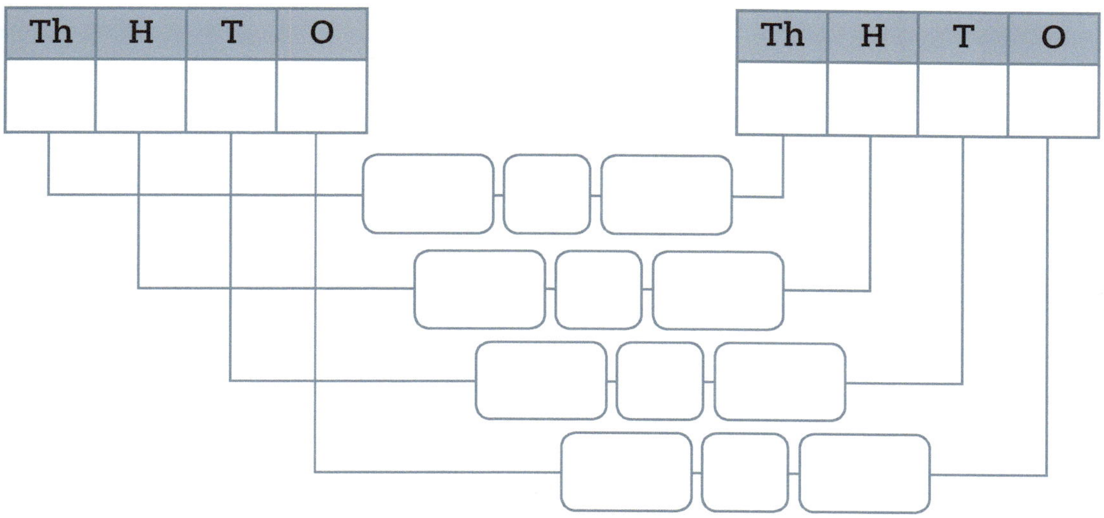

is greater.

Remember!

You can use these symbols to make comparisons:

> greater than

< less than

= equal to

b. Which number is smaller? 4,021 or 4,020?

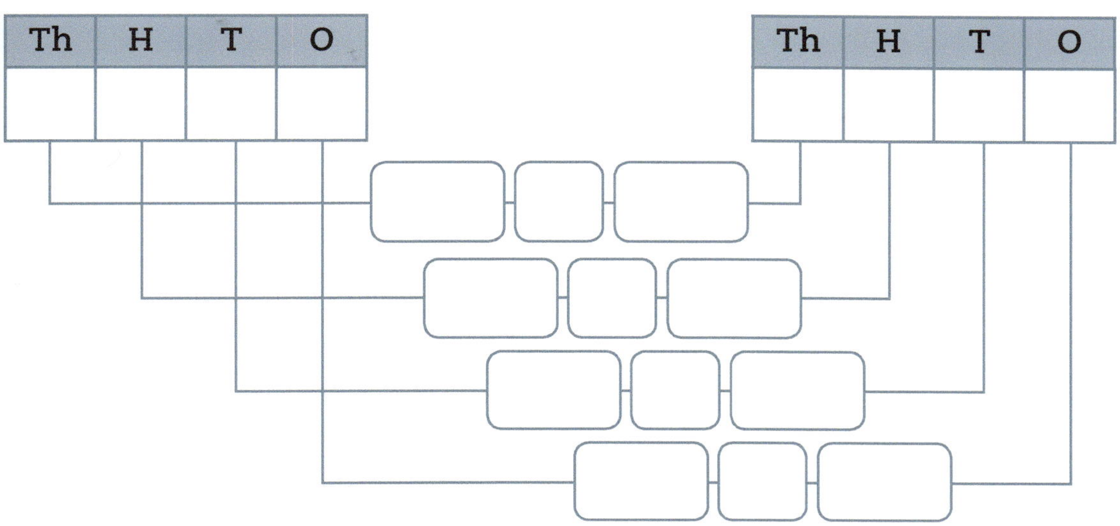

is smaller.

Comparing and Putting Numbers in Order on a Number Line

Let's Connect

Number Line

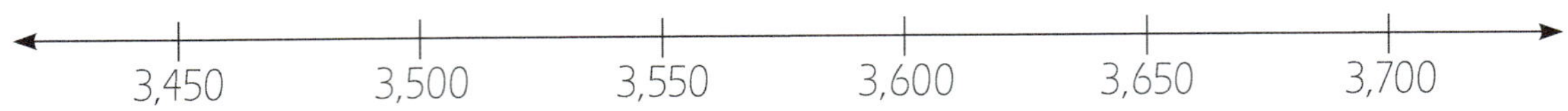

- Which is the biggest number on the number line? Write it. ☐
- At which end of the number line is the biggest number located? Circle it in .
- Which is the smallest number on the number line? Write it. ☐
- At which end of the number line is the smallest number located? Circle it in .

Did You Know...?

A **number line** is a straight line with arrows at both ends to show that it is infinite, which means it does not end.

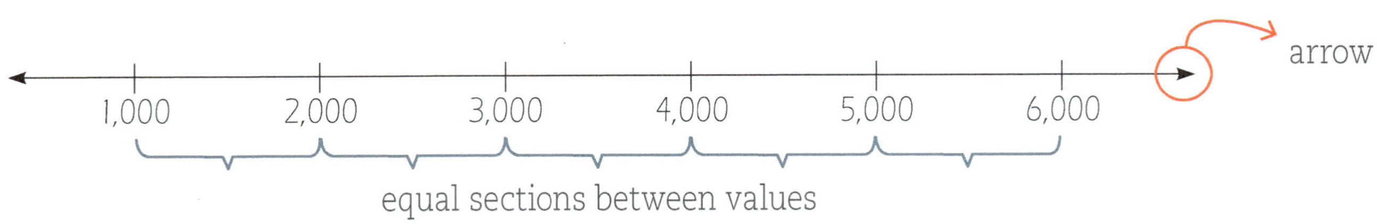

Let's Learn

To put numbers on a **number line** in **order**, first you must compare the numbers. Then, put them in order from smallest to biggest and **locate** them on the number line. Numbers to the **left** are **smaller** than numbers to the **right**.

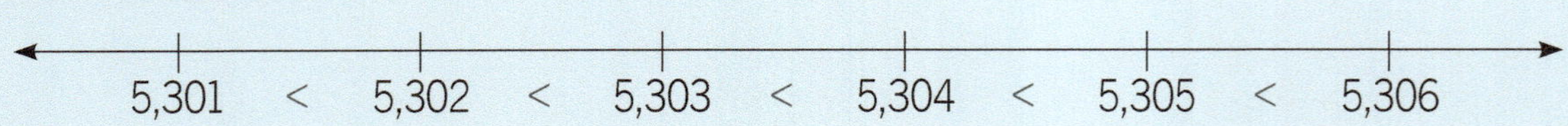

Let's Practice

1. Look at the number line and answer. Understand

6,980 6,990 7,000 7,010 7,020 7,030

a. Which numbers are bigger than 7,000? Write them.

____

b. Which numbers are smaller than 7,010? Write them.

____

c. Which is the smallest number on the number line? [ ]

d. Which is the biggest number on the number line? [ ]

2. Put each group of numbers in order on their number line. Represent

a. 1,503, 1,505, 1,502, 1,507, 1,504, 1,506

[ ] [ ] [ ] [ ] [ ] [ ]

b. 6,400, 6,300, 6,100, 6,600, 6,200, 6,500

[ ] [ ] [ ] [ ] [ ] [ ]

c. 9,370, 9,360, 9,340, 9,320, 9,350, 9,330

[ ] [ ] [ ] [ ] [ ] [ ]

Section 3

Numbers Up To 100,000

Numbers With Five Digits

Let's Connect

- How many digits does the number on the card have?

- How many TTh, Th, H, T and O does the number have?

TTh	Th	H	T	O

- How do you read the number on the card? Write it in word form.

____

____

Let's Learn

Numbers with five digits are made up of ten thousands, thousands, hundreds, tens and ones.

To read the number 41,358, say the word "thousand" after the second digit from left to right. You say "thousand" where the comma is.

Read from left to right. ⟶

Ten Thousands	Thousands	Hundreds	Tens	Ones
TTh	**Th**	**H**	**T**	**O**
4	1	3	5	8

forty-one **thousand**, three hundred fifty-eight

Let's Practice

1. Write the numbers represented by the money. Represent

a.

$

c.

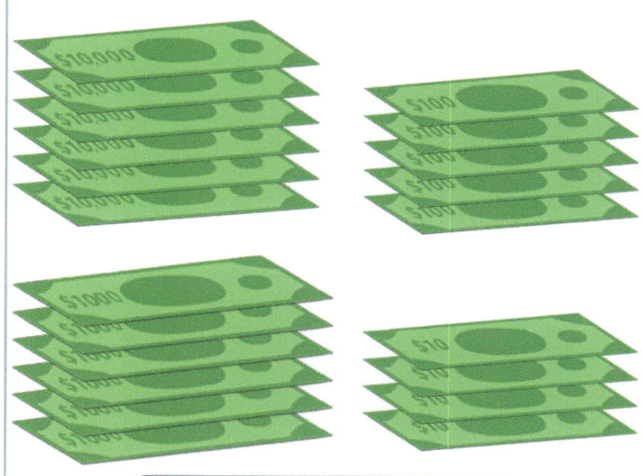

$

b.

$

d.

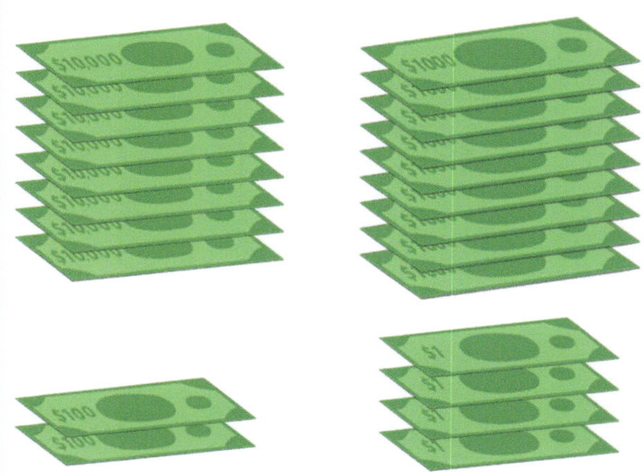

$

Education through Values

Be careful with your money. Saving money and opening a bank account will help you in the future.

2. Color the circles with the values of the TTh and Th. Recognize

a. 36,478

○ 6 Th ○ 7 TTh ○ 3 TTh ○ 8 Th

b. 58,921

○ 2 TTh ○ 8 Th ○ 5 TTh ○ 9 Th

c. 74,260

○ 0 Th ○ 6 TTh ○ 7 TTh ○ 4 Th

d. 81,888

○ 8 TTh ○ 8 Th ○ 1 TTh ○ 1 Th

3. Write the prices in word form. Represent

a. $11,990 ______________________________

b. $25,990 ______________________________

c. $44,500 ______________________________

d. $79,880 ______________________________

e. $33,333 ______________________________

4. Write the number each child says. Represent

a.

b.

c.

d.

5. Write each number in word form. Represent

a. 6 TTh, 9 Th, 1 H, 3 T, 7 O

____

b. 1 TTh, 8 Th, 6 H, 2 T, 7 O

____

c. 3 TTh, 4 Th, 6 H, 8 T, 2 O

____

d. 9 TTh, 9 Th, 8 H, 9 T, 8 O

____

Rounding

Let's Connect

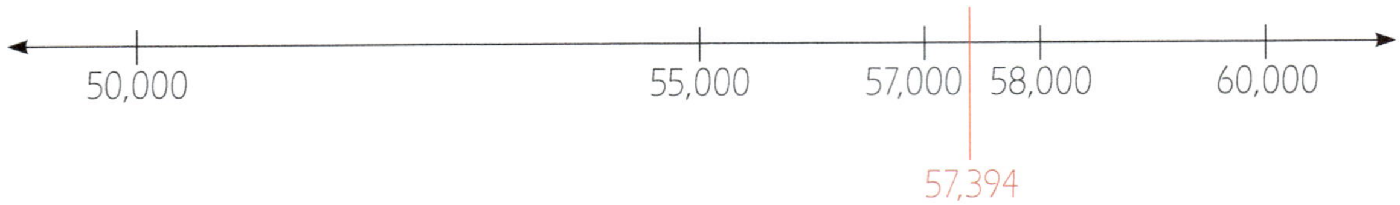

- Which number is closer to the number in red: 57,000 or 58,000?
- Which number is closer to the number in red: 50,000 or 60,000?

Let's Learn

To **estimate** is to roughly calculate an amount to obtain a quick answer. A number can be **estimated by rounding it off** to find an approximate number that has fewer digits, so that it will be easier to use.

Rounding			
to the nearest ten	**to the nearest hundred**	**to the nearest thousand**	**to the nearest ten thousand**
Look at the digit in the **ones** place. If it is equal to or greater than 5, add one digit to the number in the **tens** place. If it is less than 5, the number stays the same and…	Look at the digit in the **tens** place. If it is equal to or greater than 5, add one digit to the number in the **hundreds** place. If it is less than 5, the number stays the same and…	Look at the digit in the **hundreds** place. If it is equal to or greater than 5, add one digit to the number in the **thousands** place. If it is less than 5, the number stays the same and…	Look at the digit in the **thousands** place. If it is equal to or greater than 5, add one digit to the number in the **ten thousands** place. If it is less than 5, the number stays the same and…
…the digits to the right are replaced by zeros.			
57,394 4 < 5 57,3**90**	57,394 9 > 5 57,**400**	57,394 3 < 5 5**7,000**	57,394 7 > 5 **60,000**

Let's Practice

1. Complete the table by rounding off to the place value indicated. Follow the example. Apply

		Rounding			
	Number	to the nearest ten	to the nearest hundred	to the nearest thousand	to the nearest ten thousand
a.	45,123	45,120	45,100	45,000	50,000
b.	74,352				
c.	34,478				
d.	82,674				
e.	68,179				

Quiz Yourself

Analyze the problem and answer by rounding.

Mr. Roberts wants to buy a car that costs $89,500.

- If he pays with $10,000 bills, how many bills does he use to get the least change back?

- If he pays with $1,000 bills, how many bills does he use to get the least change back?

Calendars

Let's Connect

August						
M	T	W	T	F	S	S
			1	2	3	4
5	6	7	8	9	10	11
12	13	14	**15**	16	17	18
19	20	21	22	23	24	25
26	27	28	29	30	31	

- How many days does August have?

  It has [ ] days.

- On the calendar, why do you think the 15th is in ? Explain.

  ___

- What date is the first Friday of August?

  ___

- What day is the boy's birthday? Explain how you can calculate this.

  ___

  ___

  ___

Let's Learn

A **calendar** organizes the year into days, weeks and months. It helps us locate and organize dates and activities.

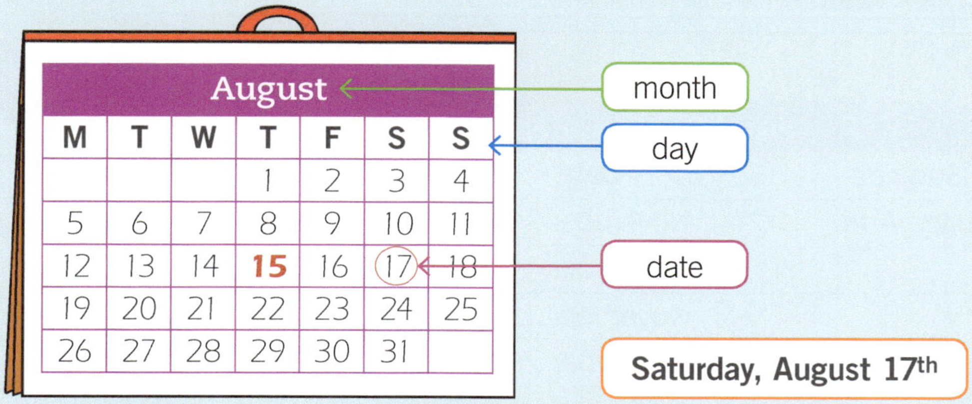

Let's Practice

1. Look at the November 2019 calendar and answer. Interpret

November						
M	**T**	**W**	**T**	**F**	**S**	**S**
				1	2	3
4	5	6	7	8	9	10
11	12	13	14	15	16	17
18	19	20	21	22	23	24
25	26	27	**28**	29	30	

a. What day is November 14th?

____

b. If Emily goes to painting classes every Saturday, how many days will she go to her painting class in November?

Emily will go to [ ] painting classes.

c. George's birthday is on November 5th, but he will celebrate it 5 days later. When will his birthday celebration be?

____

Timelines

Let's Connect

Final Exam Calendar		
Subject	**Date**	**Code**
Language Arts	November 16th	LA
Math	November 19th	M
History	November 15th	H
Social Studies	November 20th	SS

- Write the code for each subject according to the exam dates.

November					
15	16	17	18	19	20

- What is the first exam?

____

- How many days are there between the first and the last evaluation?

There are [ ] days.

- The Spanish evaluation is scheduled for November 21st, the Geography exam for November 23rd, the Biology exam two days later, and the Chemistry exam the day after that. Complete the section of calendar with the dates and exams.

November							
20							

Let's Learn

Timelines are graphic representations that put facts and events in order according to the date they happen on.
To make a timeline, you draw a horizontal line divided into equal parts. Each section represents a period of time. You then write the events and connect them to the time.

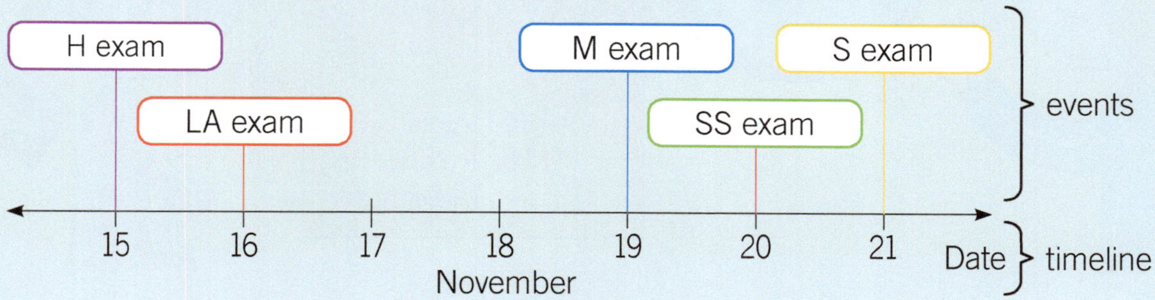

Let's Practice

1. Look at Caroline's timeline and answer the questions. Interpret

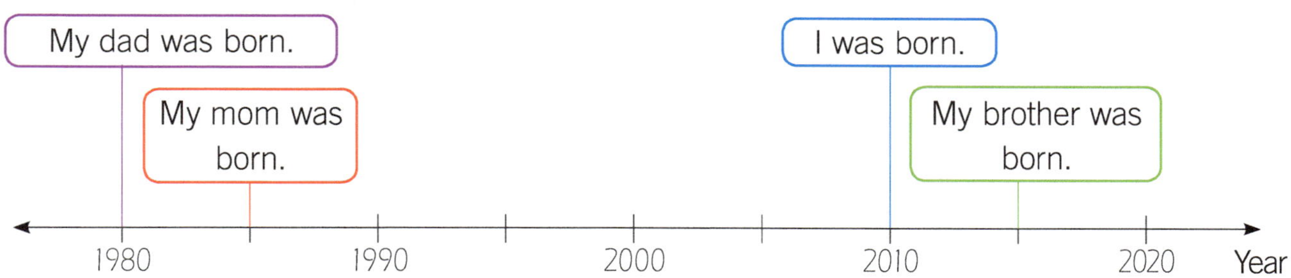

a. What year was Caroline's mom born? She was born in ☐.

b. How much older is Caroline's dad than Caroline? He is ☐ years older.

c. How old is Caroline this year? She is ☐ years old.

d. How much older is Caroline than her brother? She is ☐ years older.

2. In your notebook, make a timeline of your life. Write the events and the years you think are important. Apply

Digital and Analog Clocks

Let's Connect

- Complete the digital clocks with the time indicated.

Time when the meet starts:

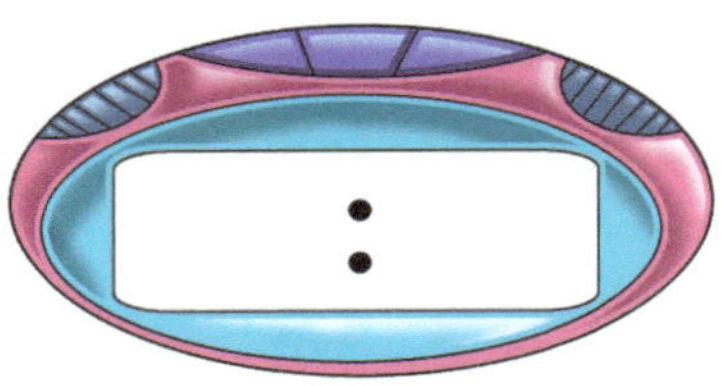

Time when the award ceremony starts:

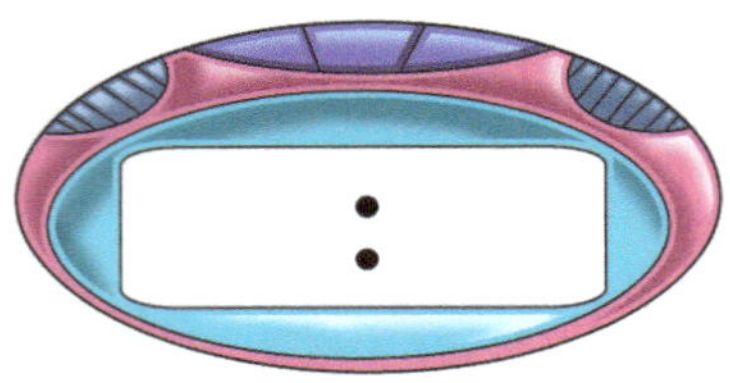

Did You Know...?

A clock with hands is called an analog clock. A digital clock uses numbers.

- What does the girl mean when she says "a quarter past"? Explain.

____

____

- What time does the clock on the wall show? Explain how you know.

____

____

- Which clock hand marks the hours? Mark it and explain your answer.

____

____

____

Let's Learn

Digital and **analog clocks** help record and show the time.

- **Digital clock:**

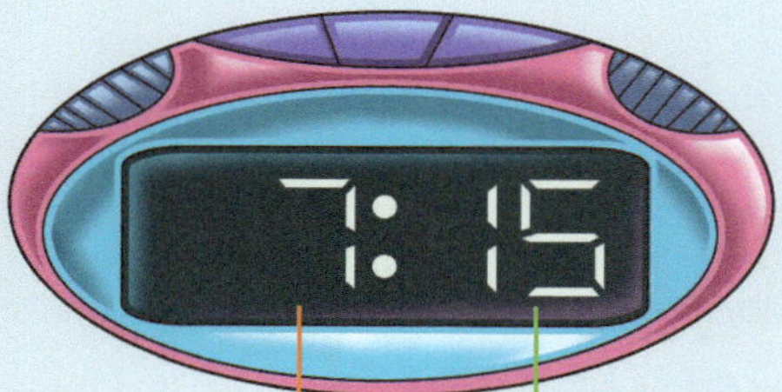

The clock shows seven hours and fifteen minutes, which we say as "seven fifteen" or "a quarter past seven."

- **Analog clocks:**
To read the time, you first look at the **shorter hand**, which indicates the **hours**. Then, you look at the **longer hand**, which indicates the **minutes**. Some clocks have a third hand that indicates the **seconds**. On the clock below, the numbers in black indicate hours and the numbers in red show how to read minutes.

The clock shows seven hours and fifteen minutes, or **seven fifteen** or **a quarter past seven**.

When the clock shows 7:15, you say "a quarter past seven" because 15 minutes is $\frac{1}{4}$ of an hour.

Tip

The short hand of an analog clock is called the **hour hand** and the long hand is called the **minute hand**.

1. Write the times shown on the clocks in word form. Interpret

a.

b.

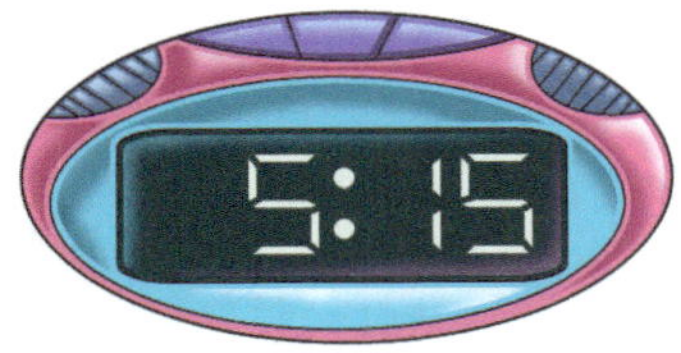

c.

2. Write the times on the digital clocks. Represent

a. ten to seven

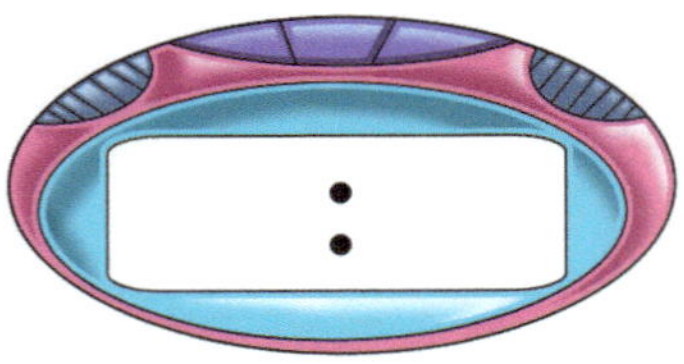

b. six twenty-five

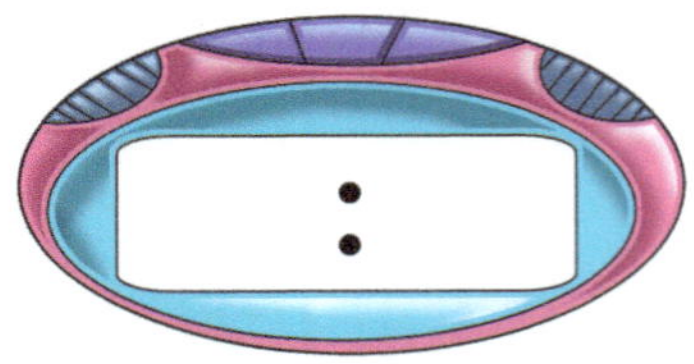

c. quarter to twelve

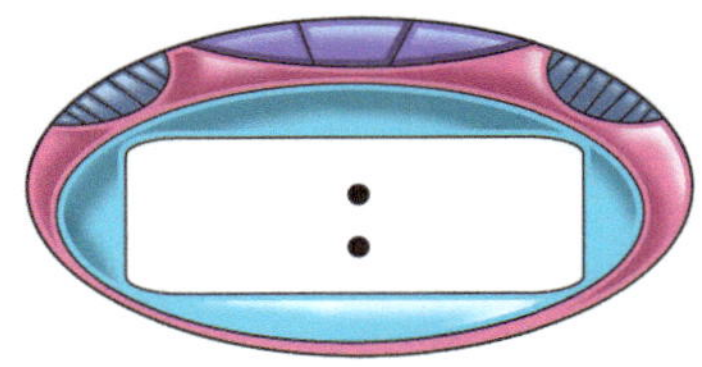

3. Match each clock with the correct time. Relate

five to nine | five past eight | eight thirty-five

4. Complete the clocks with the equivalent times. Represent

a.

b.

c.

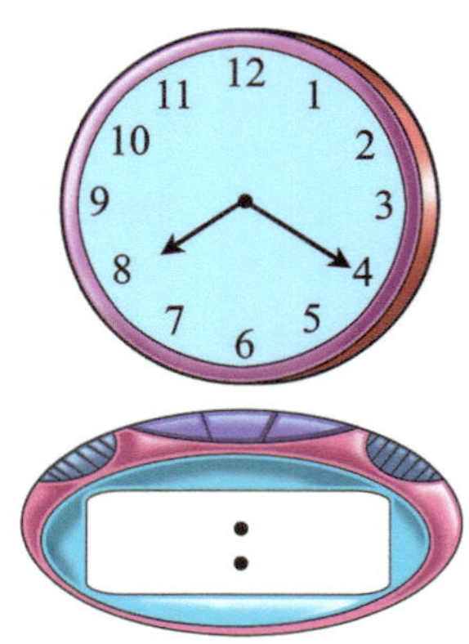

1. Draw the hands on the clocks to show the times. Interpret

a. Recess is at 10:15.

c. Classes start at 8:30.

b. Math class starts at 12:50.

d. My bus leaves at a quarter to eight.

Quiz Yourself

Analyze the problem and answer.

A plane takes off at 7:30.
The flight lasts three and a half hours.
What time does the plane arrive at its destination?

- Represent the departure time and the arrival time on the analog clocks.

departure time

arrival time

Exam Strategies

Look and Learn

Mark the correct answer with an ✕ .

1 Which number rounded to the nearest thousand equals 5,000?

- [A] 4,436
- [B] ☒ 5,436
- [C] 5,561

Read the instructions carefully.

Remember that, to round to the nearest thousand, you must look at the digit in the hundreds place.

Analyze each answer and mark the correct answer with an ✕.

Your Turn!

Mark the correct answer with an ✕ .

2 Which number rounded to the nearest ten thousand equals 20,000?

- [A] 14,990
- [B] 16,230
- [C] 25,000

What Did You Learn?

Final Evaluation

Numbers Up To 100,000

1. Write the quantities represented in numbers and in word form.

a.

$ ______ ______________________________

b.

$ ______ ______________________________

c.

$ ______ ______________________________

Place Value

2. Complete the table with the place name and place value of the digit in red in each number.

	Number	Place Name	Place Value
a.	5,147		
b.	6,842		
c.	39,175		

Comparing Using a Place Value Chart

3. Write >, < or =.

a.

Th	H	T	O
3	5	7	0

☐

Th	H	T	O
3	5	0	7

b.

Th	H	T	O
5	6	3	1

☐

Th	H	T	O
5	3	6	1

Comparing and Putting Numbers in Order on a Number Line

4. Put the numbers in order and write them on the number line.

63,488, 63,476, 63,494, 63,482, 63,500

Rounding

5. Round the numbers to the nearest thousand.

a. 87,350 ➡ ☐

b. 64,972 ➡ ☐

Digital and Analog Clocks

6. Circle the digital clock that shows the same time as the analog clock.

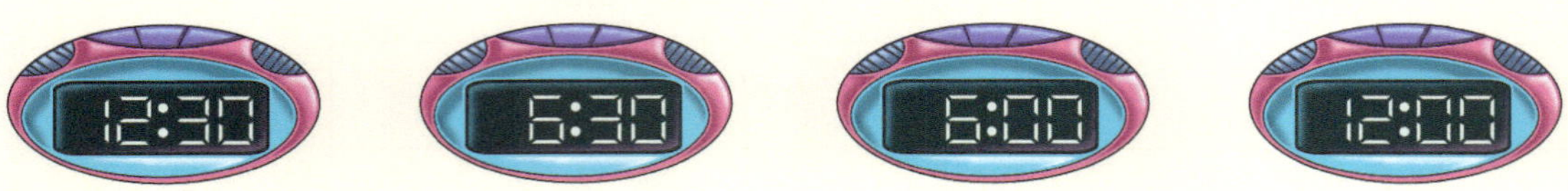

Mark the correct answer with an ✕.

Look at the number and answer questions 7–9.

TTh	Th	H	T	O
7	9	3	6	2

7. What is the decomposition of the number?

A 7 + 9 + 3 + 6 + 2

B 70,000 + 9,000 + 300 + 60 + 2

C 700,000 + 90,000 + 3,000 + 600 + 20

8. If you count by 5s starting from the number above, which is the next number?

A 79,367

B 79,372

C 79,462

9. Which number is greater than the number above?

A 79,262

B 79,361

C 79,370

Find Test 4 Study Page

How Did You Do?

For each color a .

Unit 5

Surveys and Data

Key Words

survey

Survey

Question 1
What is your favorite color?

Question 2
What is your favorite school subject?

Question 3
What sport do you play?

table

Products Bought	
Product	Price
Oranges (2 kg)	$840
Lettuces (2 heads)	$300

axis

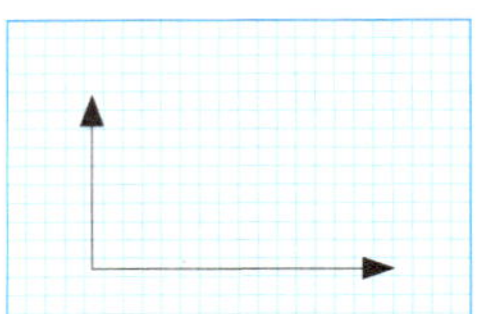

bar chart

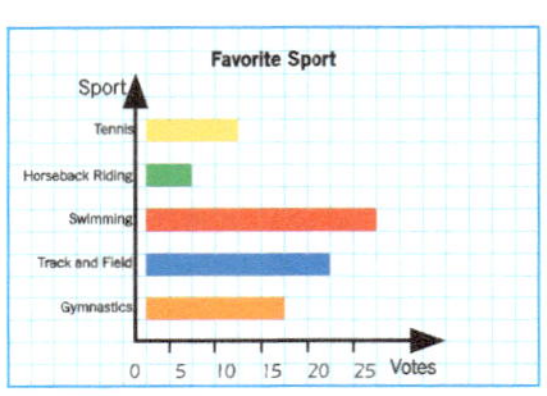

In this unit you will learn to:

- interpret and make surveys.
- organize data in tables and bar charts.
- create pictographs and bar charts with a scale.
- interpret pictographs and bar charts.
- work in an organized way.

PARENT OLYMPICS

Sport	Teams Participating
Soccer	10
Basketball	6
Volleyball	8
Handball	4

What Do You Know? Initial Evaluation

Look at the picture and answer.

1. How many sports are in the Parent Olympics?

   There are ☐ sports.

2. Which sport has the most teams?

   ____

3. Which sport has the fewest teams participating?

   ____

4. How many teams are participating in the Parent Olympics in total?

   There are ☐ teams in total.

5. What is the difference between the number of teams signed up for the least and most popular sports?

   The difference is ☐.

Section 1

Surveys, Tables and Charts

Surveys

Let's Connect

Vicky invited her friends over for dinner. Her mom asked her what kind of food she wanted her to prepare, but Vicky does not know what her friends' favorite foods are.

- What can Vicky do to find out what her friends' favorite foods are? Explain.

- How can Vicky choose the food her mom will prepare for her and her friends? Explain the steps.

Did You Know...?

A **census** is a survey of the population of an entire country.

Let's Learn

We use surveys to **collect data** or the **opinions** of a group of people. A **survey** allows you to find information by asking people simple questions.

For example, you can do a survey of your classmates to find out their favorite food by asking the question "What is your favorite food?" and recording the answers.

Let's Practice

1. Analyze each situation. Write the questions that ask for the information. Analyze

a. Ingrid wants to know how many kids in her class can swim.

Question: ______________________________

b. John wants to organize a competition, but he does not know which sport to pick.

Question: ______________________________

c. Sara wants to know how many teachers in her school play sports.

Question: ______________________________

2. Create a survey with three questions you can ask your classmates. Create

Survey

Question 1

____

Question 2

____

Question 3

____

Education through Values

Using information collected through a survey can help make decisions more democratic. It gives everyone the opportunity to express their preference or opinion on a subject.

Data in Tables and Bar Charts

Let's Connect

Analyze the information from a survey represented in the table and the bar chart.

What is your favorite color?

Table

Favorite Color	
Color	**Votes**
Yellow	2
Green	1
Red	5
Blue	4

Bar Chart

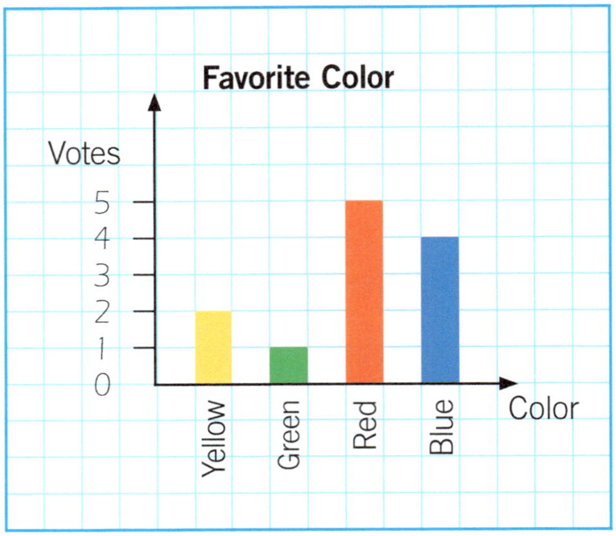

- What is the survey about? Who do you think made the survey?

  ____

- Which are the colors with the most and the fewest votes?

  ____

- Which representation shows the responses to the question more clearly, the table or the bar chart? Why?

  ____

  ____

- If each person answered the survey once, how many people were surveyed?

  ____

Let's Learn

Tables allow you to **organize** and put the **information** or **data** from a survey **in order**.

Favorite Color	
Color	**Votes**
Yellow	2
Green	1
Red	5
Blue	4

When data is organized in tables you can compute different calculations, such as finding the total number of people surveyed, and you can present the information clearly.

Bar charts also allow you to visualize survey data clearly.

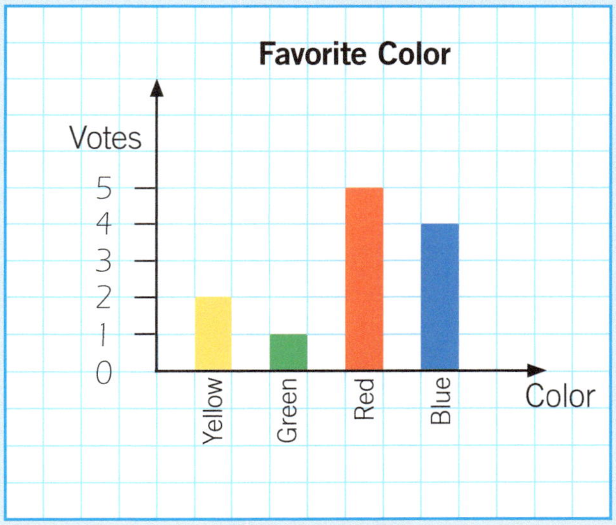

When data is presented in a bar chart you can identify information quickly by looking at the length of the bars.

Let's Practice

1. Read the descriptions. Write "table" or "bar chart". Recognize

a. It often uses color to represent information. __________

b. It has rows and columns. __________

c. It has bars that represent information. __________

d. It is easy to identify data and compute different calculations. __________

2. Read the survey carefully. Then, organize the data in the table and represent it in a bar chart. Organize

To organize a class party, a teacher surveyed her students to find out what their favorite juice was. The answers she got were: 8 students like strawberry juice, 7 students like orange juice and 5 students like mango juice.

Favorite Juice Flavor	
Flavor	**Votes**
Strawberry	
Orange	
Mango	

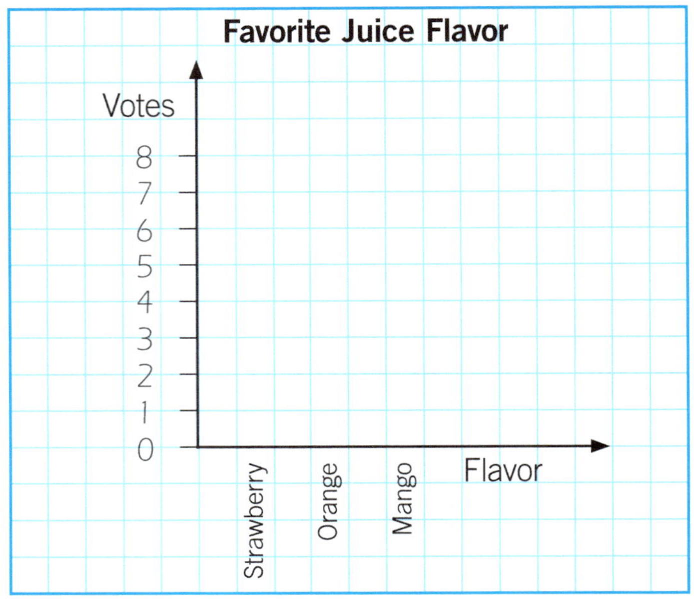

Tip

Bar charts are often easier to read when there is a space between each bar.

3. Look at the data in the table and the bar chart. Answer. Analyze

a. Which is the most popular juice? ______________________

b. How many students like mango juice? [ ]

c. What is the difference between the most and the least popular juices? [ ]

d. If each student answered only once, how many students answered the survey? [ ]

Education through Values

Sharing information about yourself with your classmates allows you to get to know them better and find things you have in common.

Quiz Yourself

Analyze the information and make a bar chart that represents it.

A survey of a third grade class found this information:

- The most popular after-school activity is playing sports.
- The least popular after-school activity is watching television.
- The two other options in the survey, reading and listening to music, were equally popular.

In total, 20 students were surveyed. Half of the 20 students had the same preference and only 2 chose watching television.

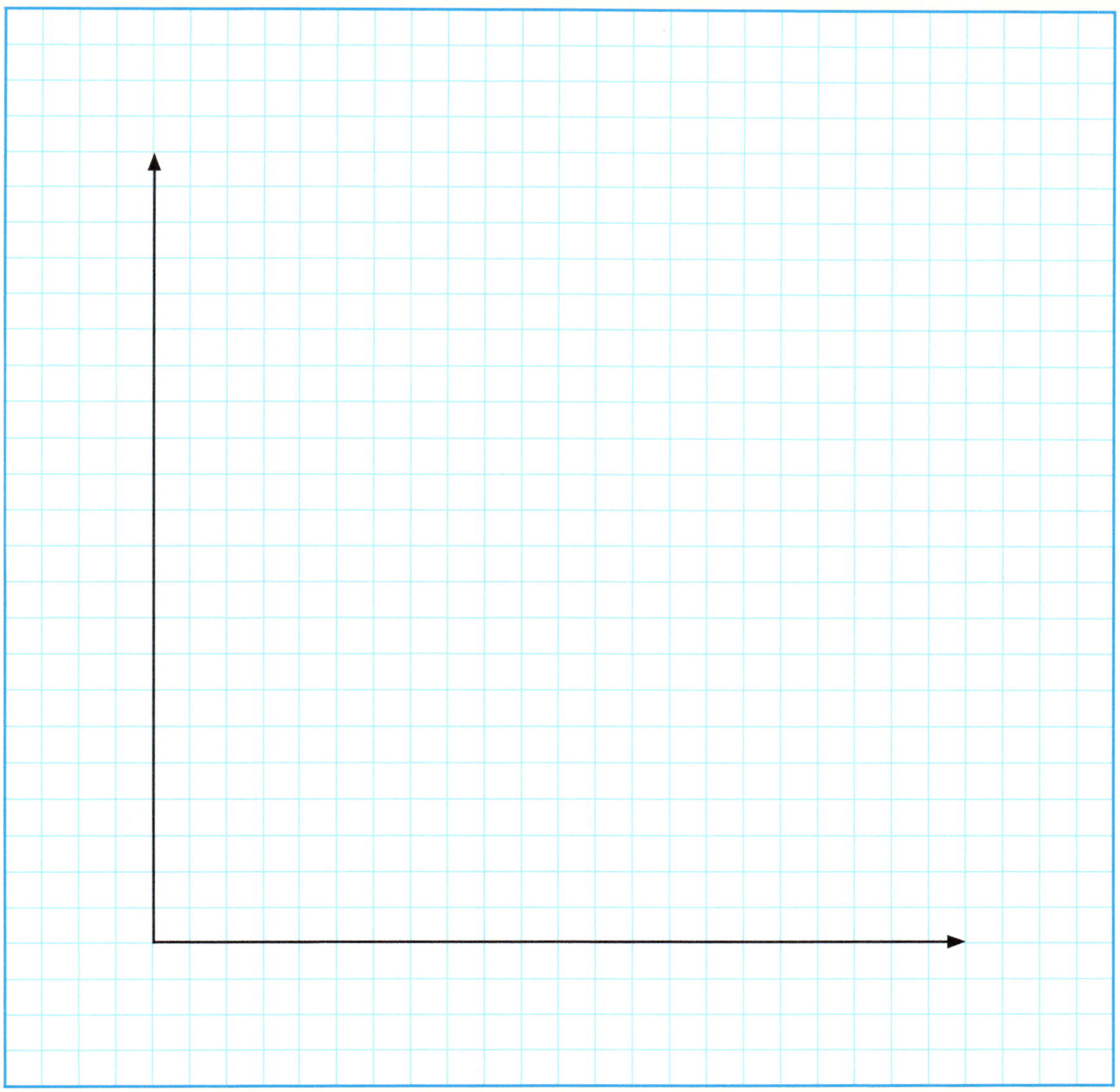

Section
2 Making Pictographs and Charts

Making Pictographs With a Scale

Let's Connect

Pictograph 1

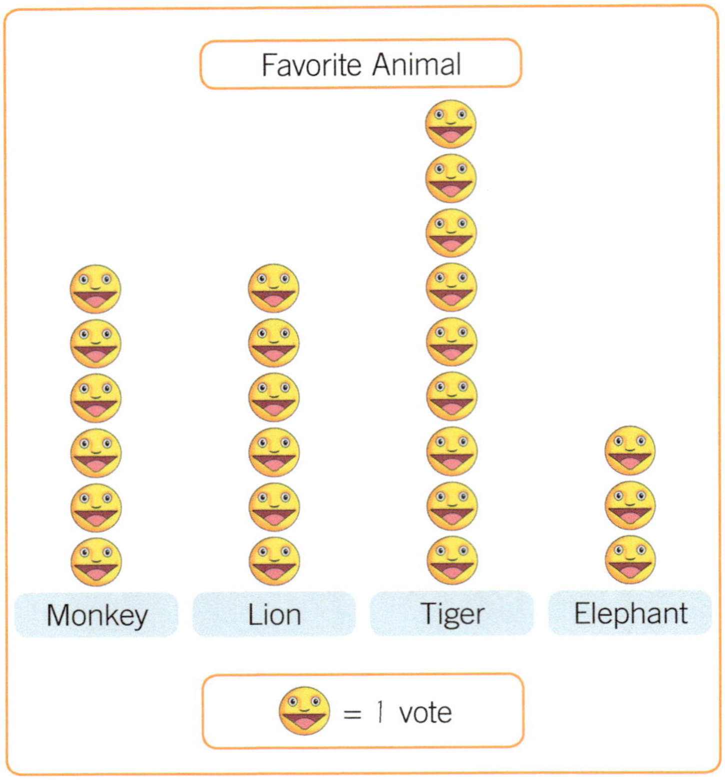

Pictograph 2

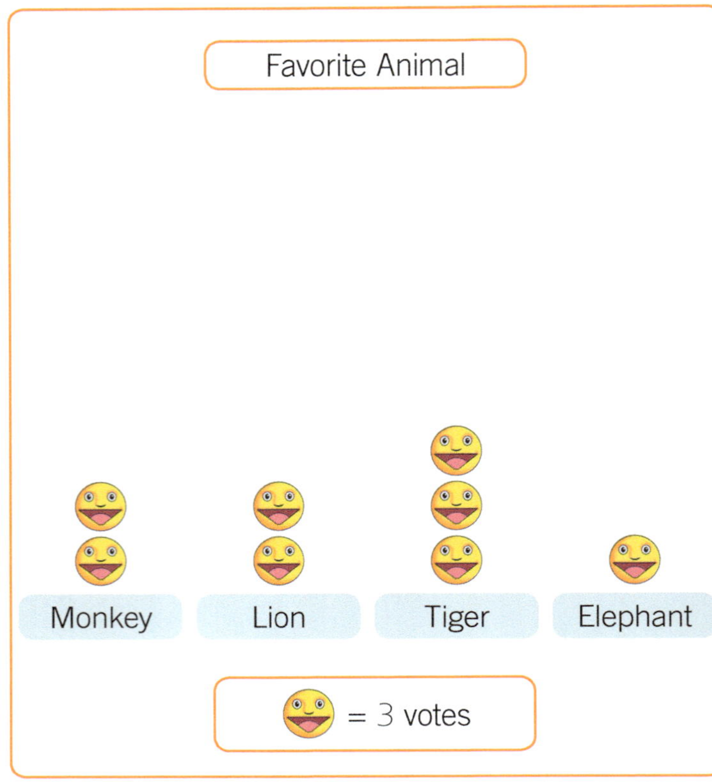

- Complete the table with the differences and similarities between the pictographs.

Pictograph 1	Pictograph 2
Differences	
Similarities	

Let's Learn

A **pictograph** is a type of representation where you use pictures or symbols to represent the data from a survey.

The picture or symbol used in the pictograph is usually related to the topic. It represents a specific **amount** or the **scale** of the pictograph.

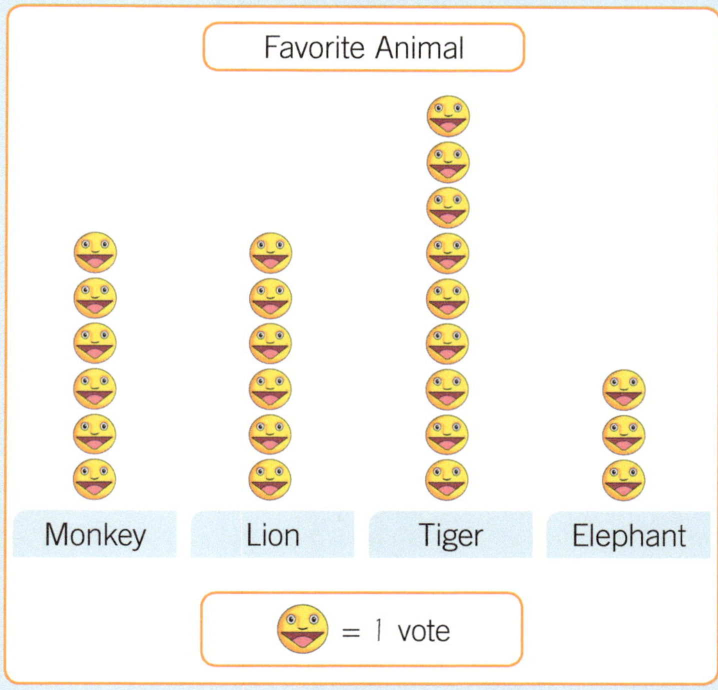

In this pictograph, the number that the symbol represents is 1. So, the **scale** is 1.

Remember that pictographs have a title related to the data in the chart.

Use scales greater than one when there is a lot of data. This will make representing the information easier.

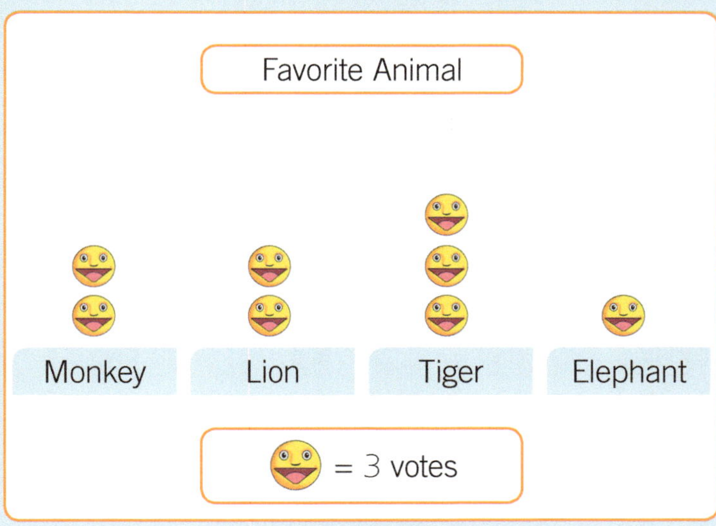

In this pictograph, the number that the symbol represents is 3. So, the **scale** is 3. This means that one equals 3 votes.

Let's Practice

1. Represent the data from the table in a pictograph. Color 1 apple for every 5 kg of fruit. Represent

The table shows how many kilograms of fruit a store sells daily for a week.

Fruit Sold Daily							
Day	Monday	Tuesday	Wednesday	Thursday	Friday	Saturday	Sunday
Quantity (kg)	15	10	20	15	20	50	25

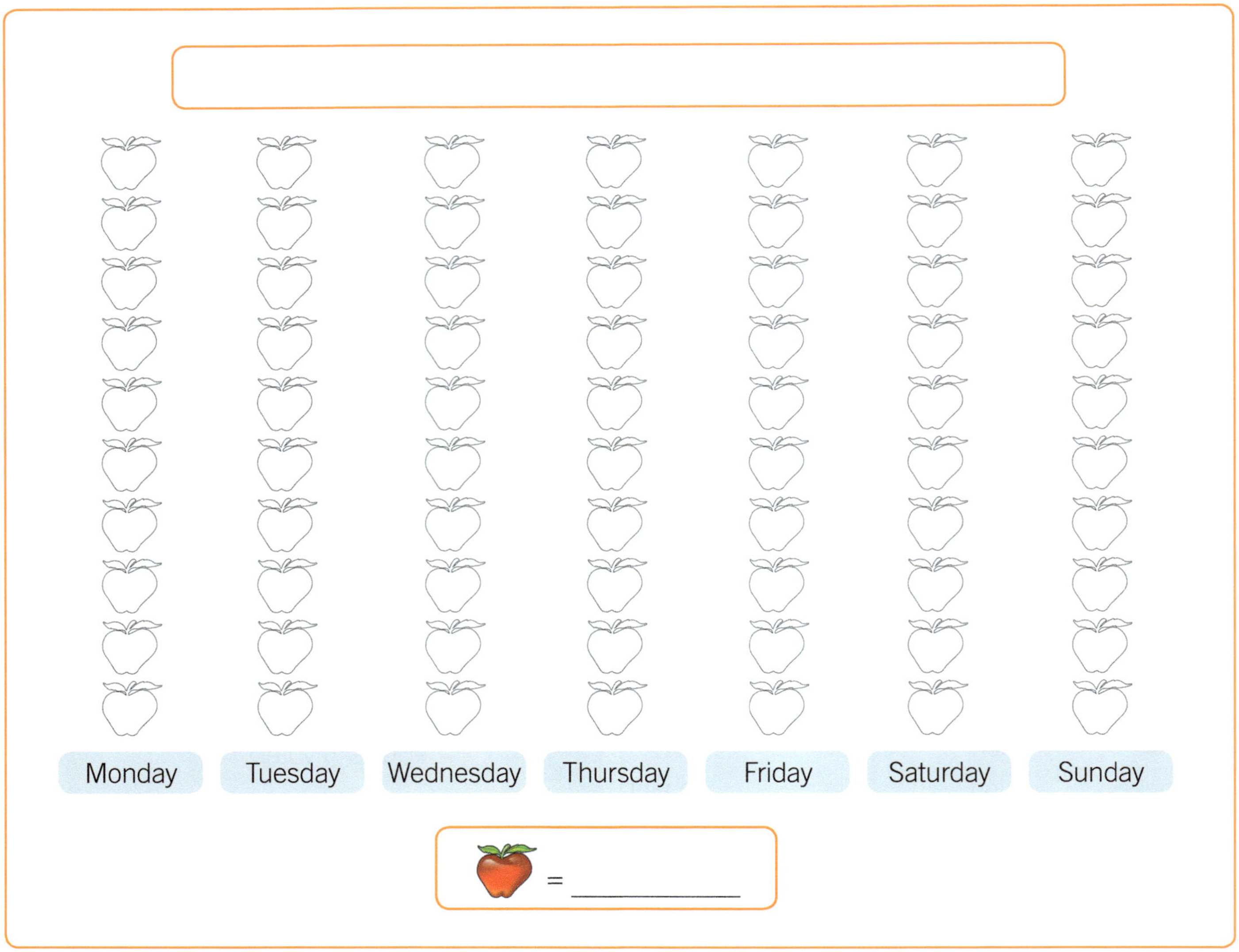

2. Represent the data in a pictograph. Choose a symbol and decide the best scale. Analyze

A farm has:

24 sheep	12 horses	18 ducks	9 cows	27 chickens

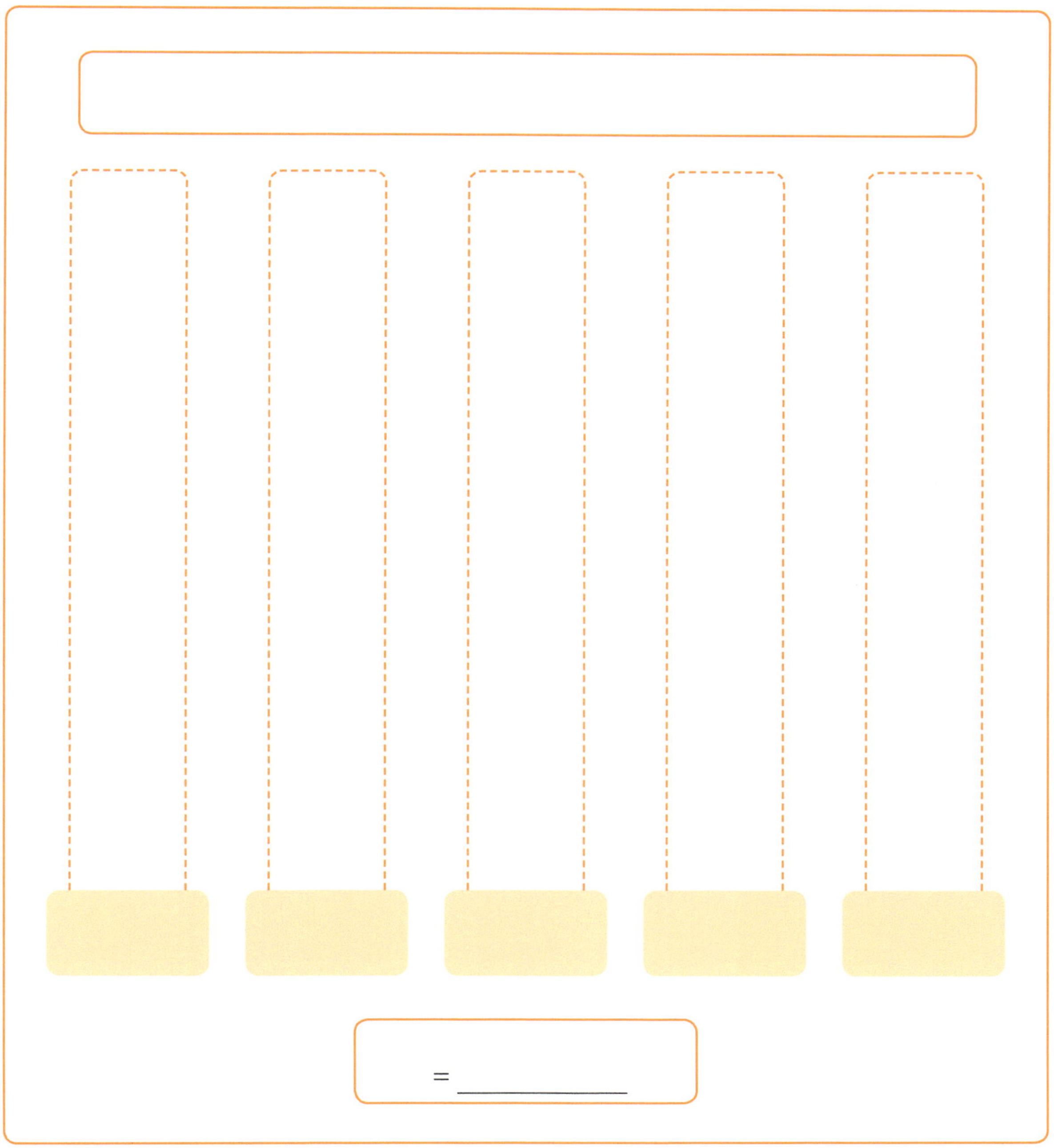

Making Bar Charts With a Scale

Let's Connect

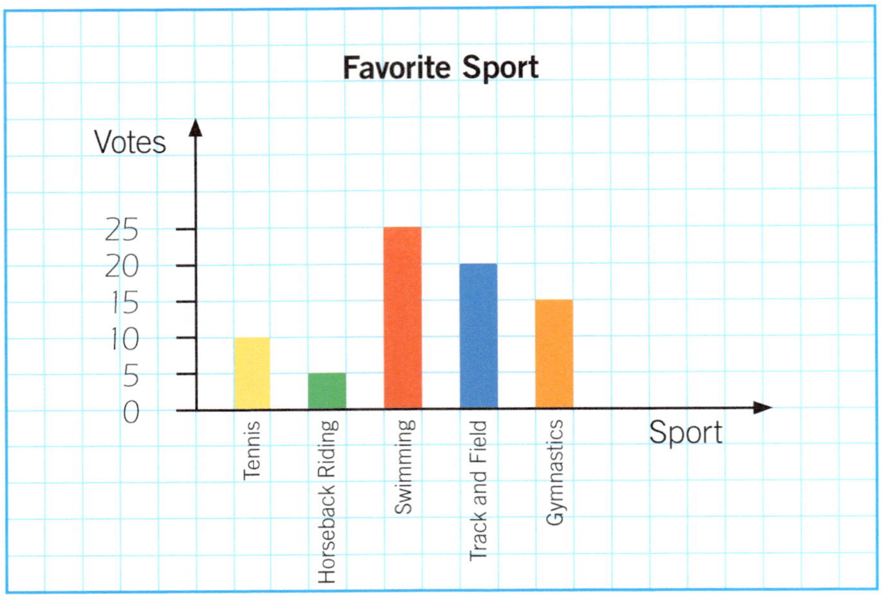

Tip

A bar chart usually has these parts: a title, two axes, labels for the axes, variables or categories and rectangular bars.

- What is the title of the bar chart?

____

- What are the names of the axes? Explain what they mean.

____

- How many bars does the chart have?

It has ☐ bars.

- How many people like each sport? Complete.

Tennis	Horseback Riding	Swimming	Track and Field	Gymnastics
☐	☐	☐	☐	☐

- What is the scale of the "Votes" axis?

____

Let's Learn

When making a **bar chart with a scale**, remember to include all the necessary information.

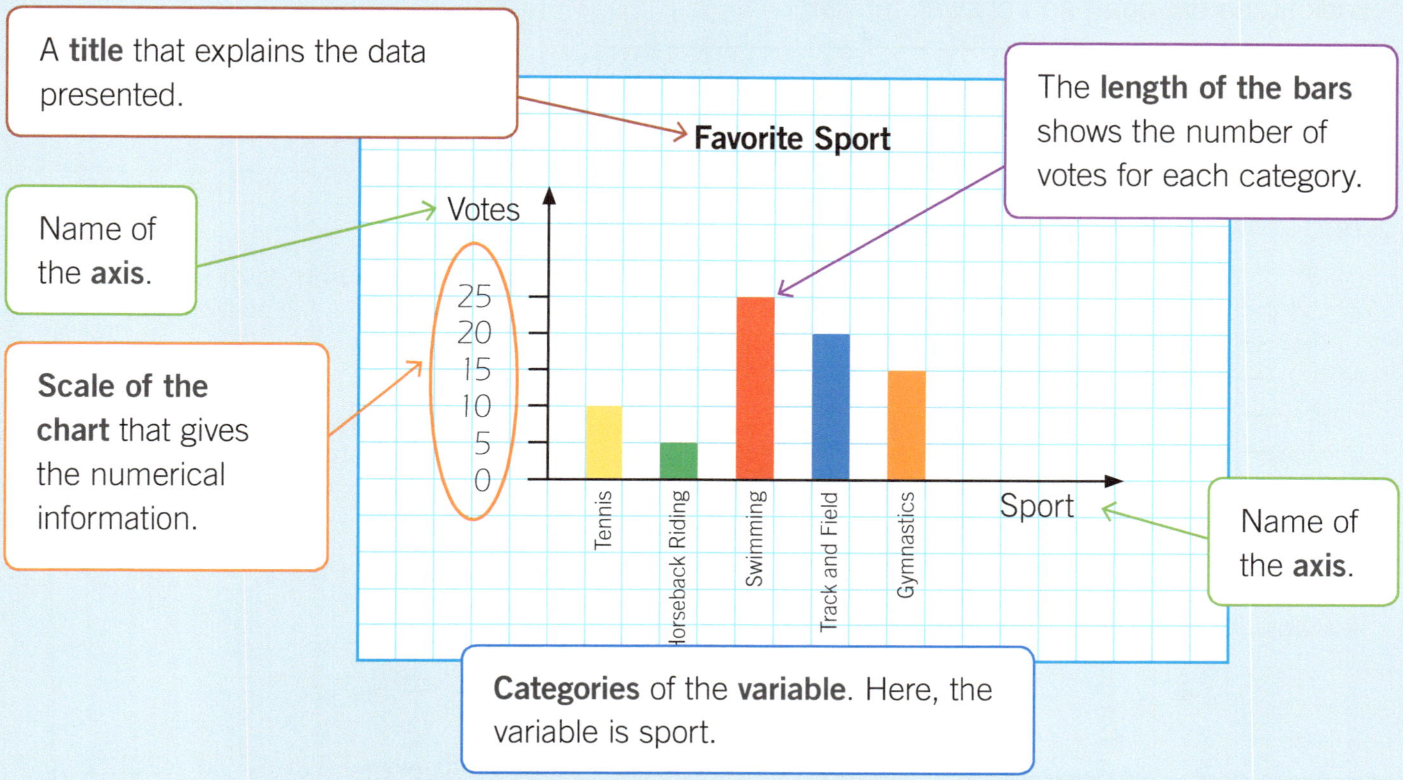

A bar chart can be horizontal or vertical, depending on the direction of the bars.

Vertical Bar Chart

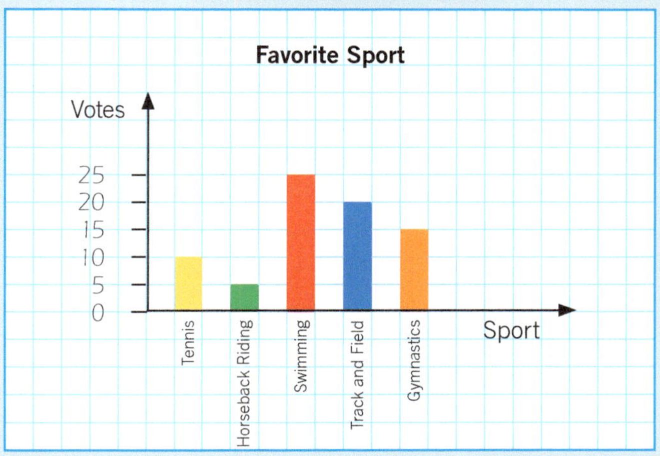

Horizontal Bar Chart

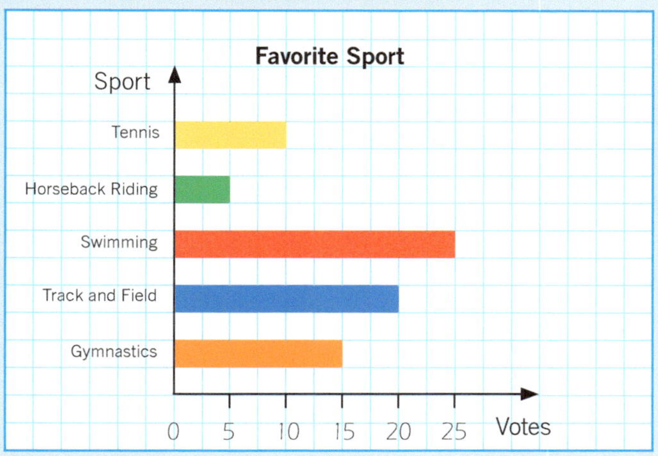

Remember that the **axes** must have a scale that starts at 0 and that can be counted in equal segments. Here, the bar charts have a scale of 5.

Let's Practice

1. Look at the bar chart and answer. Interpret

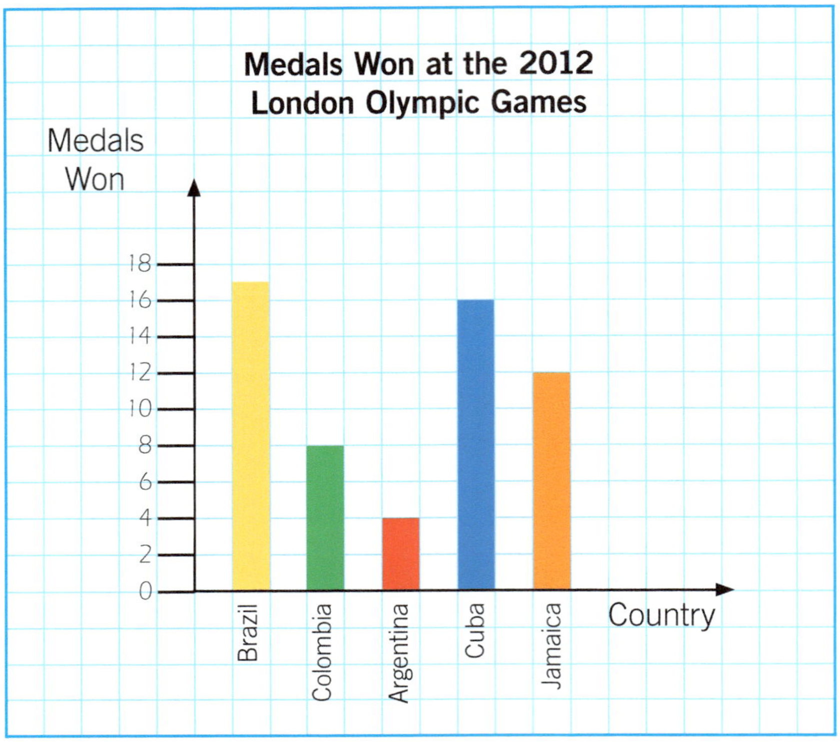

a. What is the title of the bar chart?

____

____

b. What are the names of the axes?

____

____

c. What is the bar chart's scale?

____

Source: http://www.juegosenlondres2012.com

2. Represent the data in the table in a horizontal bar chart. Use a scale of 2. Represent

Medals Won by Russia at London 2012			
Medals	Gold	Silver	Bronze
Number	24	26	32

Source: http://www.juegosenlondres2012.com

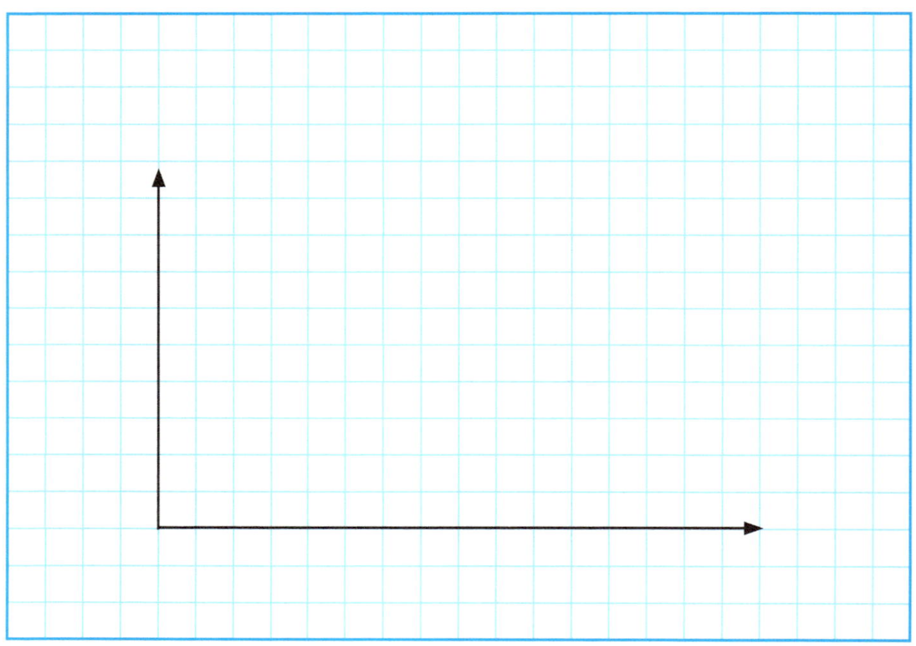

3. Read the information and represent it in a vertical bar chart. Remember to include all of the elements of a bar chart and use the scale that you think works best. Represent

A group of people answered a survey about their favorite vacation destination. These were the answers:

- 10 people prefer the countryside.
- 5 people prefer the mountains.
- 25 people prefer the beach.
- 20 people prefer a different country.

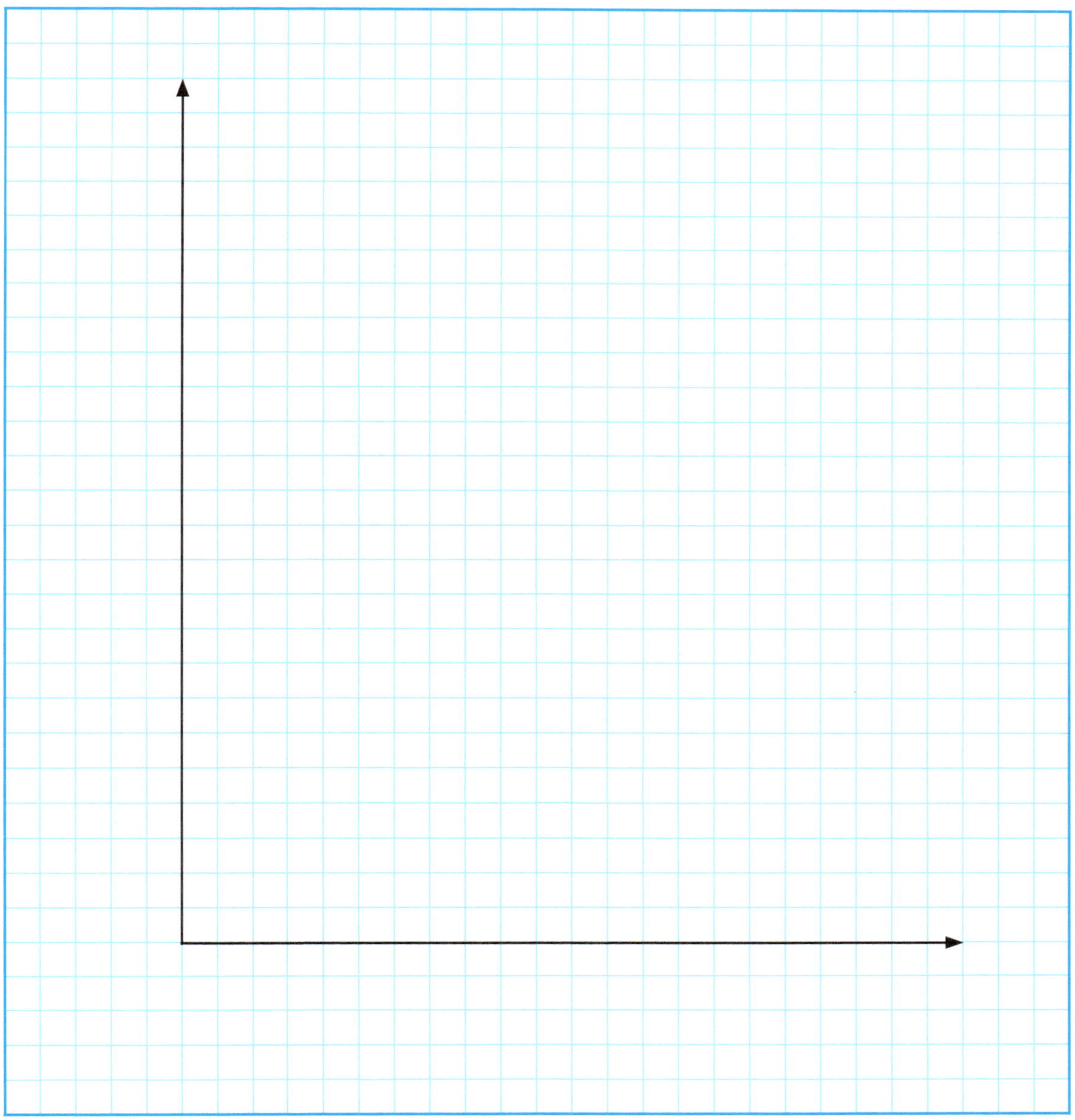

4. Represent each set of data in a bar chart. Represent

a. Louise is a gymnast. She trains Monday to Saturday. The number of hours she practices each day are shown in the table.

Daily Hours of Training						
Day	Monday	Tuesday	Wednesday	Thursday	Friday	Saturday
Hours	3	3	4	2	2	5

b. In a recycling campaign, third graders filled bags with plastic bottles.

Bags Filled by Each Class				
Class	3A	3B	3C	3D
Bags	8	10	6	3

Quiz Yourself

Analyze the problem and answer.

A third grade teacher wants to motivate her students to maintain the good grades they had this semester. She has the information in a table.

Grade Averages		
	Last Name	**Average**
1	Ahrens	7.5
2	Alvarez	8.7
3	Brown	8.5
4	Danielson	7.3
5	Faulkes	9.3
8	Griffin	8.5
7	Lee	8.3
8	Nardi	7.4
9	Okamura	8.4
10	Patzer	7.5
11	Pederson	8.5
12	Reyes	8.7
13	Ross	9.4
14	Roth	8.5
15	Rymill	8.8
18	Simpson	9.0
17	Soto	8.5
18	Tena	8.7
19	Thomas	7.8
20	Tran	8.7

- Represent the data in a bar chart with the title “Students’ Grade Averages.”

Let's Check!

Data in Tables and Bar Charts

Use the information to answer questions 1 and 2.

To know what her students like to do in their free time, a teacher made a survey. The results were: 7 students like to read, 5 like to listen to music, 6 like to play sports and 2 like to watch TV.

1. Represent the data in a table.

2. Represent the data in a bar chart.

Making Pictographs with a Scale

3. Represent the data in the table in a pictograph. Add a title, and color one Flour for each 5 kg of flour.

Daily Flour Production				
Mill	Fields	Red Barn	The Getaway	Sunnydale
Amount (kg)	25	35	15	20

How Did You Do?

For each face color a lily pad.

Section 3

Interpreting Pictographs and Charts

Interpreting Pictographs with a Scale

Let's Connect

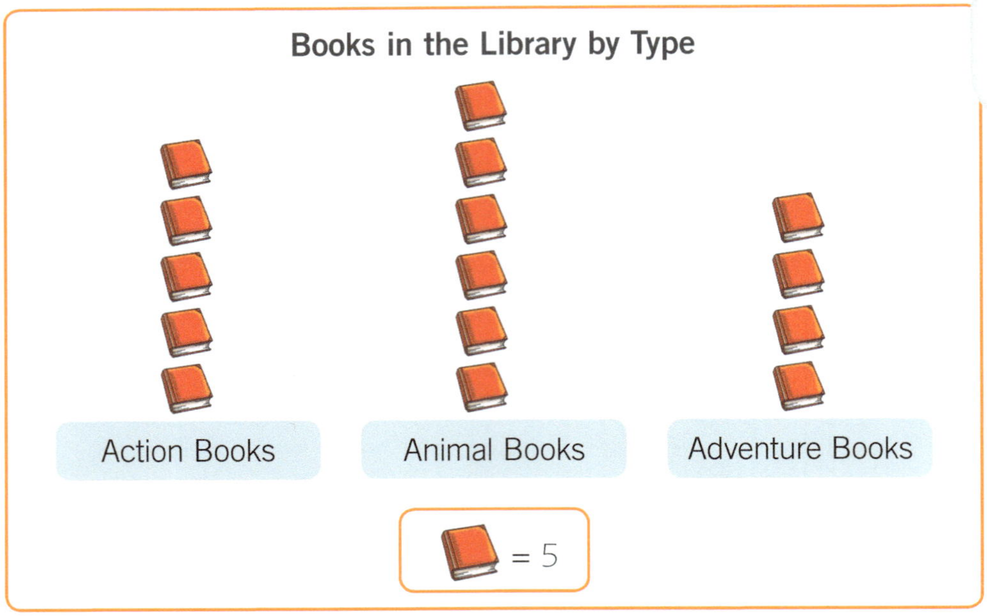

- How did Ann know there were 30 books about animals in the library? Explain.

____

____

- Which type of book is there the fewest of? How many are there?

____

Let's Learn

To **interpret a pictograph with a scale** you must know the scale and the categories of the variable you are studying. This data will help you understand the information in the pictograph.

For example, in the "Books in the Library by Type" pictograph, each  represents 5 books in the library. Therefore, there are 25 action books, 30 animal books and 20 adventure books.

Let's Practice

1. Mark the information you can obtain from this pictograph with a ✔. Understand

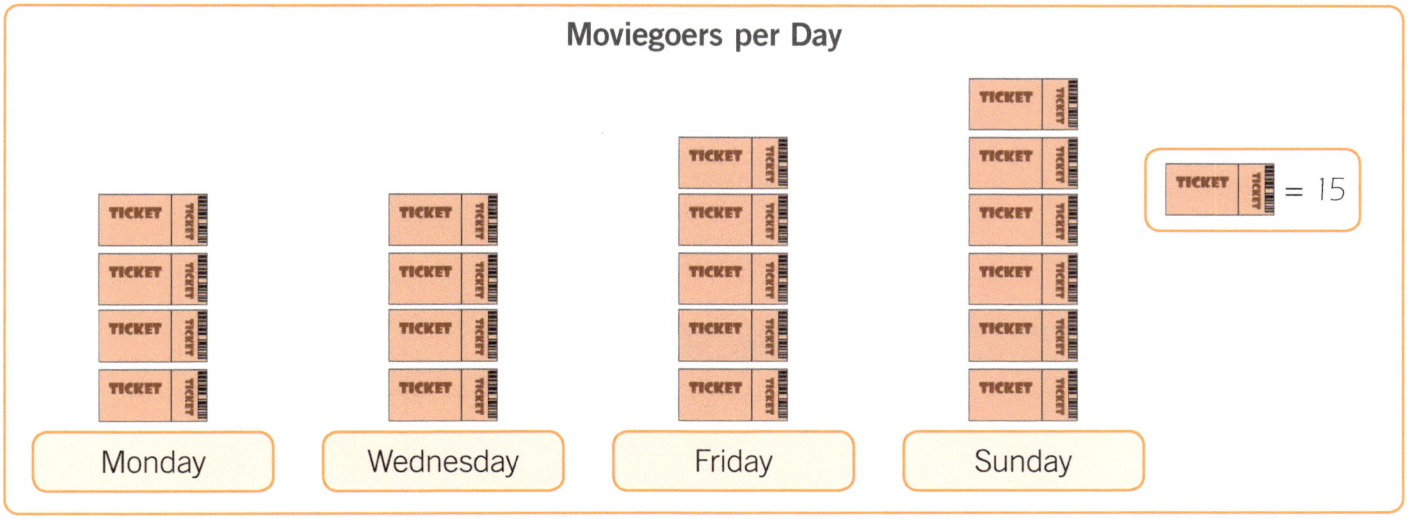

a. ◯ The day with the most moviegoers was Sunday.

b. ◯ On Monday, 30 people were seated and 30 were standing.

c. ◯ On Friday, there were 15 more people than on Wednesday.

d. ◯ The same number of men as women went to the movies.

2. Write three conclusions you can make from the pictograph. Analyze

____

____

____

____

____

____

____

____

Interpreting Bar Charts with a Scale

Let's Connect

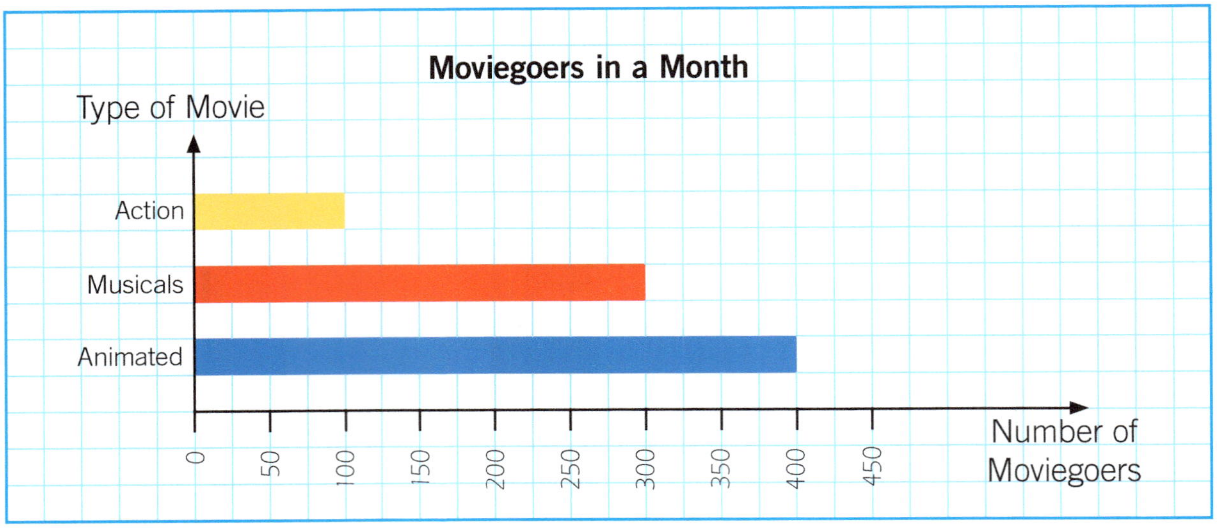

- What is the scale of the horizontal axis?

____

- Which type of movie had the fewest moviegoers? Which had the most?

Fewest	Most
_______________	_______________

- What is the relationship between the length of each bar and the variables on the vertical axis? Explain.

____

____

Let's Learn

To **interpret a bar chart with a scale**, first identify the scale being used to record the data. This way, you can relate the length of each bar to the variables on the other axis.

For example, in the bar chart "Moviegoers in a Month," the scale is counted by 50s. The length of each bar indicates that the least popular type of movies are action movies with 100 moviegoers. The most popular are animated movies with 400 moviegoers.

Let's Practice

1. Use the bar chart to answer the questions. Interpret

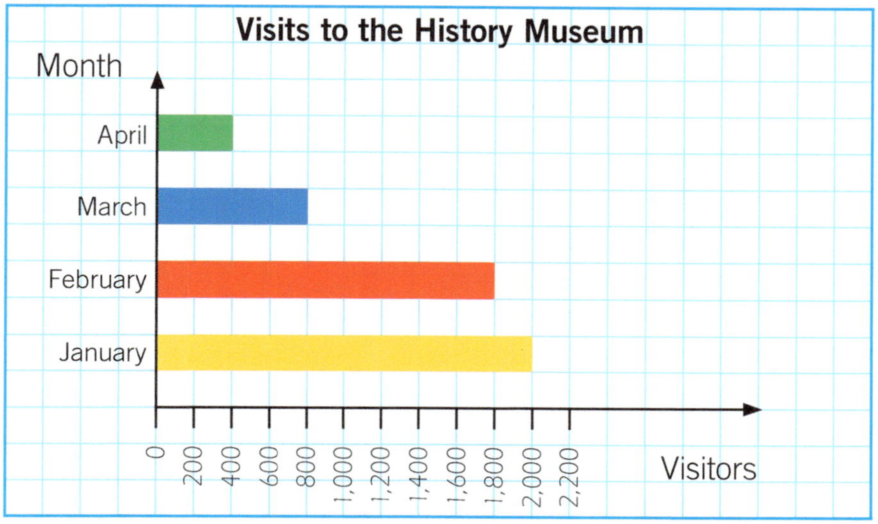

a. Which was the month with the fewest number of visitors? Which had the most visitors?

Fewest	Most
______________	______________

b. By what amount did the visitors increase or decrease between January and February, and between February and March? Calculate.

Between January and February: __________ Between February and March: __________

c. The tickets are always the same price. If ticket sales are donated to a children's home, in which month did the home receive the biggest donation?

____

d. Why do you think the amount of visitors decreases as the months pass by? Explain.

____

____

2. Interpret the problem and answer. Interpret

A third grade teacher surveyed her students about what transportation they use to get to school. Then she recorded the data in the bar chart.

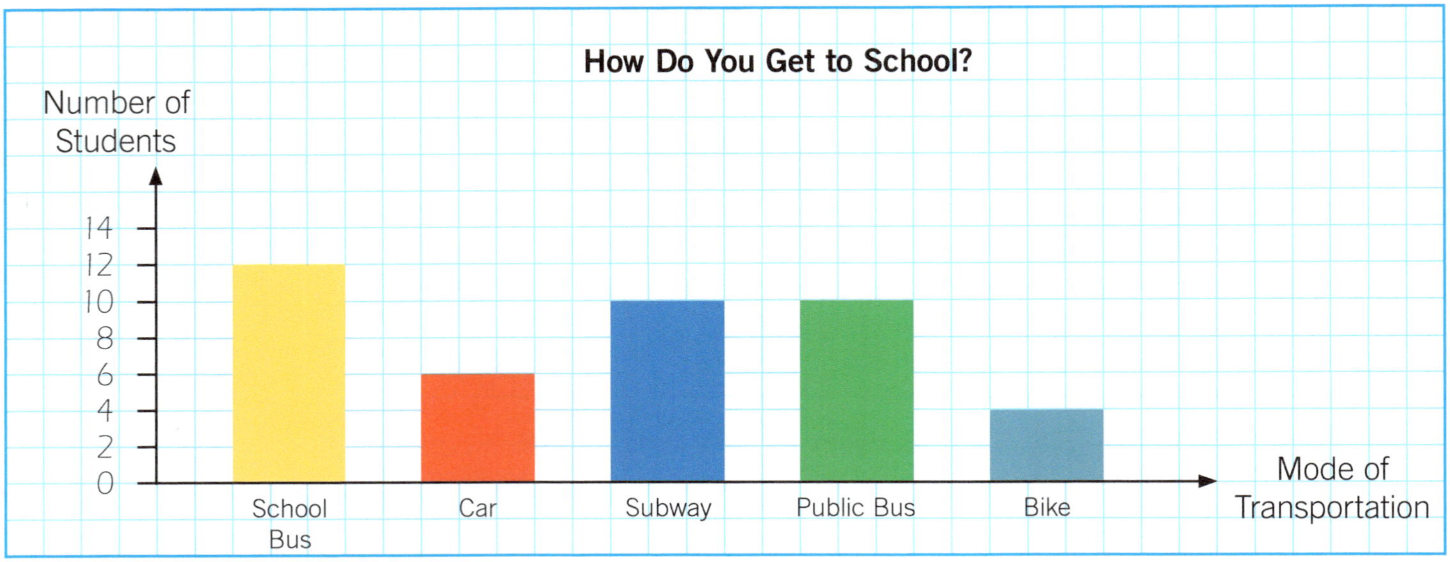

a. What information is represented in the bar chart?

____

b. What is the most common mode of transportation used by the students in the group?

____

c. What is the least common mode of transportation used by the students in the group?

____

d. Why do you think only four students use a bike as a way to get to school?

____

e. If each student answered only once, how many students did the teacher survey?

The teacher surveyed ☐ students.

Quiz Yourself

Analyze each representation. Then, answer.

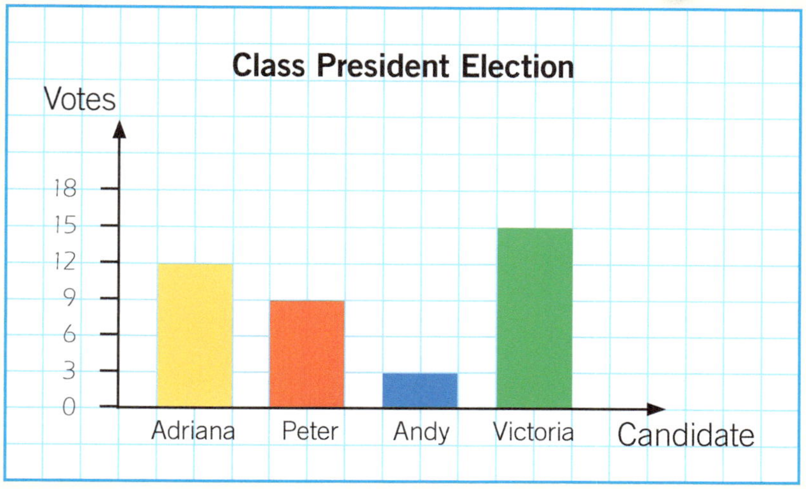

- According to the information from both representations, how many votes does the ✔ symbol represent in the pictograph?

  ____

- Name one difference and one similarity between the representations.

  Difference: ______________________________

  Similarity: ______________________________

- Which student was chosen as class president?

  ____

- If each student voted once, and one student did not vote for any of his classmates, how many students voted in total?

In total, ☐ students voted.

Exam Strategies

Look and Learn

Mark the correct answer with an ✗.

1 The bar chart shows the results of a survey about a group of children's favorite colors. According to the chart, how many children answered the survey?

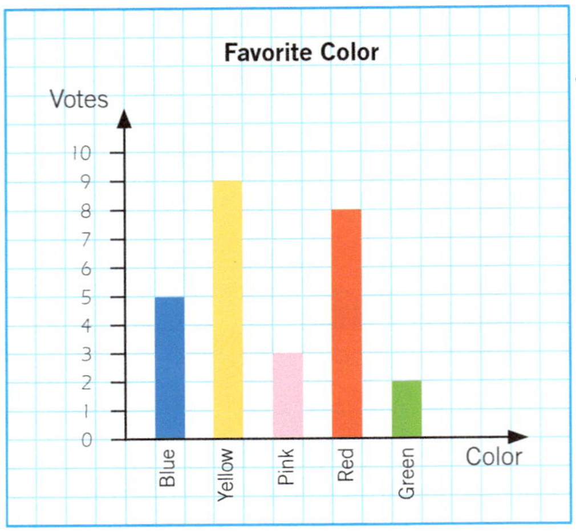

Read the instructions carefully.

To answer, interpret the chart by remembering what the different elements mean. Identify the scale that is used and interpret the meaning of the length of the bars.

A 9 | B 12 | ☒ C 27 | D 30

Look for the correct answer.

Your Turn!

Mark the correct answer with an ✗.

2 The bar chart shows the number of shirts sold in a store in five days. How many shirts were sold in total during the five days?

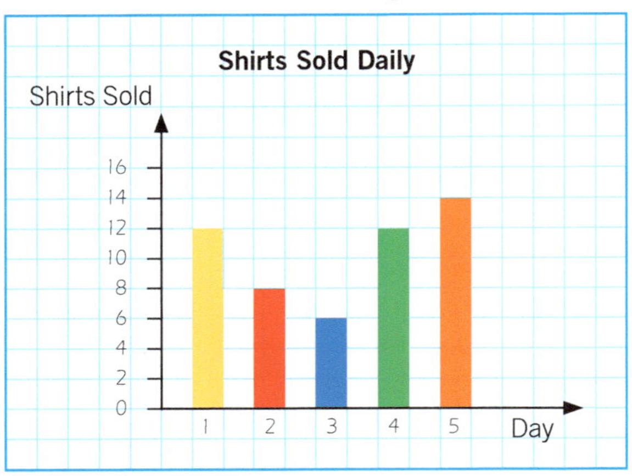

A 13 | B 15 | C 52 | D 57

What Did You Learn?

Making Bar Charts with a Scale

Use the information to answer questions 1 and 2.

Jeff travels to different cities for his job. The amount of work trips he made in the last few months are shown in the table.

Jeff's Work Trips	
Month	**Trips**
December	5
January	3
February	1
March	6

1. Represent the information from the table in a horizontal bar chart. Use the scale you think is best.

2. Look at the bar chart above. Answer the questions.

   a. How many trips did Jeff make between December and March?

   ____

   b. In which month did Jeff make the most trips?

   ____

3. Use the information in the pictograph and write **T** if the statement is **true** and **F** if it is **false**. Explain.

a. ☐ In March, they sold two more bicycles than in June.

____

b. ☐ In May, they sold 40 bicycles.

____

c. ☐ In April, they sold 10 bicycles less than in June.

____

d. ☐ In June they sold 30 bicycles.

____

e. ☐ Between March and June they sold 140 bicycles in total.

____

Mark the correct answer with an ✕.

Use the information from the pictograph and answer questions 4 and 5.

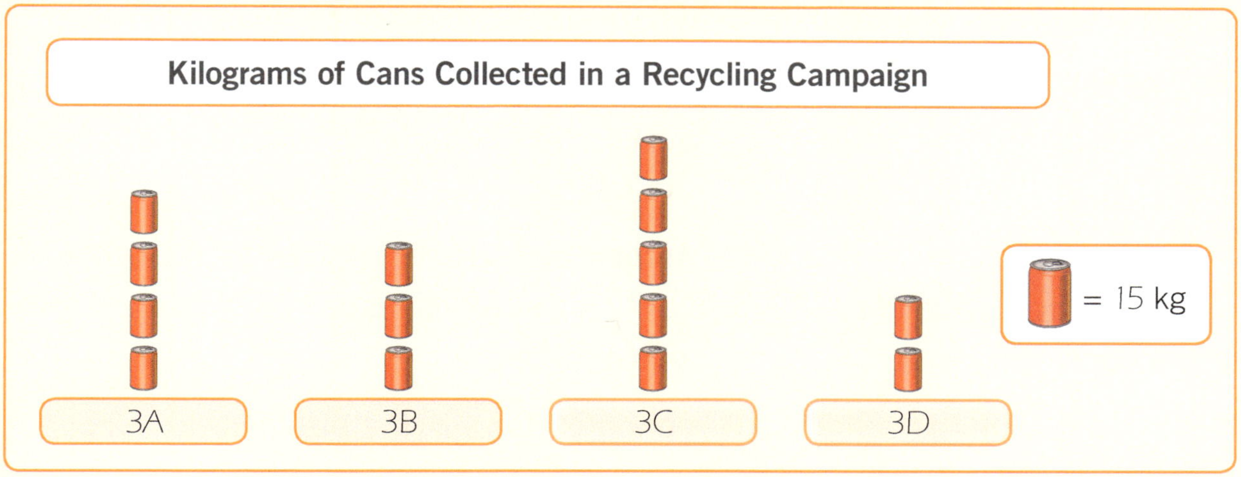

4. Which grade collected the most cans?

- **A** 3A
- **B** 3B
- **C** 3C
- **D** 3D

5. Which answer puts the number of cans each grade collected in order from greatest to least?

- **A** 3D, 3B, 3A, 3C
- **B** 3C, 3A, 3B, 3D
- **C** 3C, 3B, 3A, 3D
- **D** 3D, 3A, 3B, 3C

Find Test 5 Study Page

How Did You Do?

For each color a .

Glossary

3.1 Key Words Unit 1

pattern – *n*, the regular and repeated way in which something happens or is done

hundreds chart – *n*, a diagram that shows numbers from 1 to 100 and multiplication and number patterns

operation – *n*, a math process; addition, subtraction, multiplication and division

equality – *n*, the state of having the same quantity, size or measurement

unknown – *n*, a number that is not known, represented by a symbol or a letter

3.2 Key Words Unit 2

grouping – *n*, an arrangement of things into equal groups

equal distribution – *n*, the characteristic of having the same amount of something in different places

multiplication term – *n*, a word used to describe a component of a multiplication operation

repeated element – *n*, something that appears two or more times

3.3 Key Words Unit 3

whole – *n*, all, everything, the total amount; the denominator in a fraction

part – *n*, a portion of the whole, a piece of the total amount; the numerator in a fraction

numerator – *n*, the number at the top of a fraction that signals how many parts of the whole there are

denominator – *n*, the number at the bottom of a fraction that signals the total parts of the whole

grid – *n*, a system of intersecting straight lines that form evenly divided squares on a piece of paper, a map, etc.

3.4 Key Words Unit 4

place value chart – *n*, a chart that divides the digits of a number into their place values

number line – *n*, a line representing numbers with marks showing values

timeline – *n*, a line that includes marks showing when particular events happened in the past

calendar – *n*, a document, chart, etc., that shows the days, weeks and months of a year

3.5 Key Words Unit 5

survey – *n*, a method of gathering information

table – *n*, information organized in columns and rows

axis – *n*, a fixed line used for showing measurements or finding the position of points on a graph

bar chart – *n*, a chart that uses rectangles to represent numbers

A

above – *adv*, in or to a higher place

add – *v*, to put two or more numbers together to find a total or sum

addend – *n*, a number that is added to another

analog clock – *n*, a clock that shows the time using rotating hands (long parts that move in a circle) that point to numbers

appropriate – *adj*, especially suitable or fitting to a particular situation

arrow – *n*, a mark to show direction

B

backward – *adv*, toward the back or the beginning

balance – *v*, to arrange so that one set of elements exactly equals another

below – *adv*, in or to a lower place

C

category – *n*, a group of people or things that have similar qualities

census – *n*, a counting of the population of a place

coordinate – *n*, any of a set of numbers and letters used to locate a point on a line or surface or in space

court – *n*, a space for playing a ball game

cheap – *adj*, not expensive

coin – *n*, a flat round piece of metal with special designs on it, used as money

compare – *v*, to find the differences or similarities between things. Use these symbols to compare: >, <, =

composition – *n*, a way to write numbers using digits from 0 to 9

corral – *n*, the fenced area where livestock animals are kept

D

dairy – *n*, foods that are made from milk, for example butter and cheese

data – *n*, information collected and used to understand ideas or topics

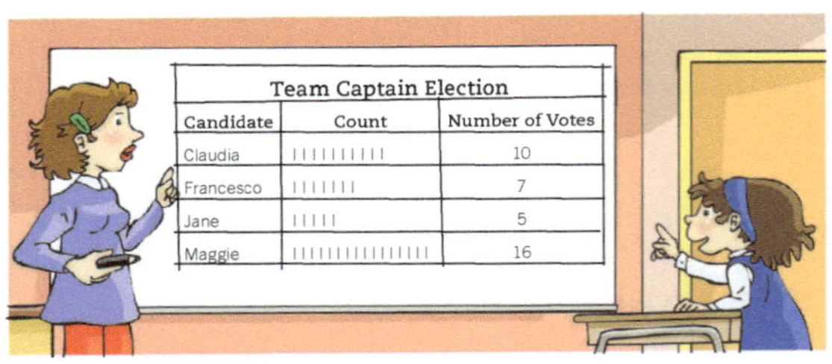

decomposition – *n*, a way to write numbers by showing the value of each digit

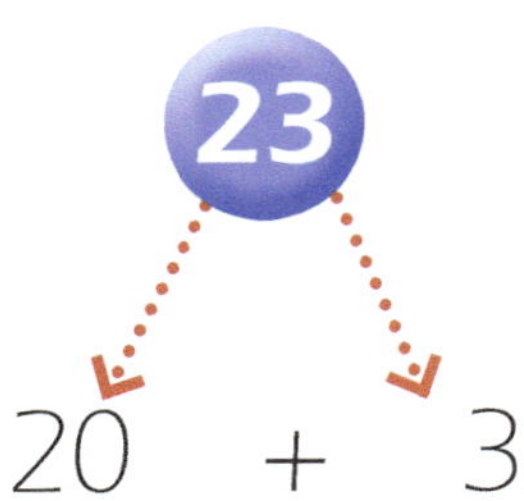

decrease – *v*, to reduce or become less

democratic – *adj*, having to do with democracy; believing in equal rights

diagonal – *n*, a straight line joining opposite corners

die – *n*, a small, six-sided block of wood or plastic marked with dots, that you roll or throw to play a game

difference –*n*, something that makes one thing or person not the same as another thing or person

digit – *n*, any of the numerals from 0 to 9

digital clock – *n*, a clock that shows information as a row of numbers

direction – *n*, the line or course along which something moves, lies or points

display – *v*, to put something in a particular place so that people can see it easily

double – *v*, to cause (something) to become two times as great or as many

E

end – *n*, the final part of something

equal – *adj*, the same in number, amount, degree, rank or quality

equivalent – *adj*, with the same size, value, importance or meaning as something else

estimate – *v*, to give or form a general idea about the value, size or cost of (something)

F

factor – *n*, a number that you can divide a larger number by exactly

$$\underbrace{9 \times 8}_{\text{factors}} = 72$$

forward – *adv*, toward the front or end

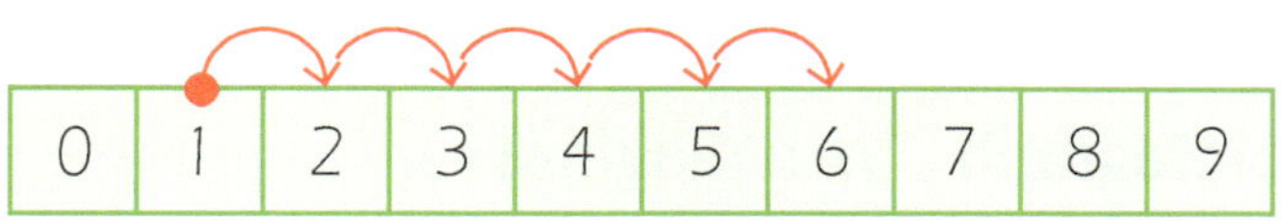

fraction – *n*, a representation of a part of a whole or, more generally, any number of equal parts

fraction bar – *n*, the line that separates the numerator and the denominator in a fraction

G

greater than – *adj*, more than, larger than

grid – *n*, evenly divided squares on a piece of paper, a map, etc.

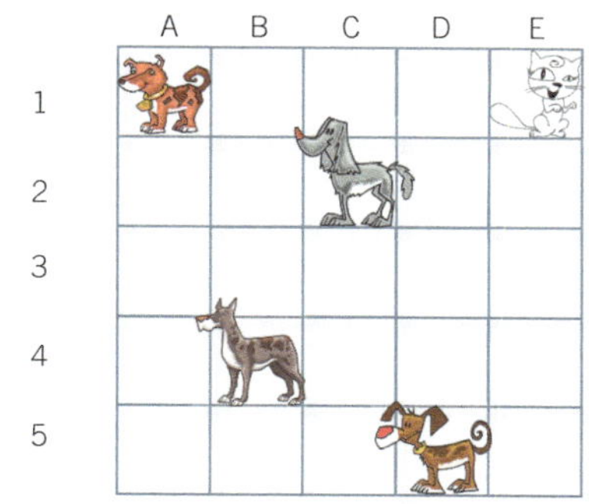

H

half, halves (pl) – *n*, one of two equal parts into which an amount, group or object can be divided

horizontal – *adj*, parallel to the horizon

hour hand – *n*, the moving part that points to the hour on a clock or watch

I

increase – *v*, to become larger in amount or number

infinite – *adj*, having no limits or boundaries

K

known value – *n*, a number generally recognized

L

leap year – *n,* a year that has one extra day in the month of February every four years

least – *adj,* smallest in amount or degree

left – *adj,* of, relating to, situated on or being the side of the body in which the heart is located

length – *n,* the distance from one end of something to the other end

location – *n,* a place or position

M

measurement – *n,* the exact size, degree, strength etc. of something, usually expressed in numbers of standard units

minute hand – *n,* the moving part on a clock or watch that points to the number of minutes past the hour

multiplication table – *n,* a list that shows the results of multiplying certain numbers by each other

N

near, nearest – *adj,* used for referring to the side of something that is the closest to where you are

numeral – *n,* a symbol that represents a number

O

ordinal number – *n,* a number that shows what position something has in a series

P

pack – *n,* a set of things such as products wrapped or tied together

past – *adv,* used for saying what time it is when it is not more than thirty minutes after one, two etc. o'clock

pen – *n,* a small area where farm animals are kept

pictograph – *n,* a diagram representing statistical data by using simple pictures

place value – *n,* the value assigned to a digit within a number, based on its location in that number

plate – *n,* a flat and usually round dish that is used for eating or serving food

point of reference – *n,* information that you already have that helps you to understand a new situation

position – *n*, where something is in relation to other things

product – *n*, the result when two numbers are multiplied

Q

quarter – *n*, one of four equal parts into which something can be divided; one-fourth

R

repeated addition – *n*, adding a number to itself more than one time

4 + 4 + 4

right – *adj*, of, relating to, situated on or being the side of the body which is away from the side on which the heart is located

Roman numeral – *n*, one of the letters that were used by the ancient Romans to represent numbers, and that are still used today

I II III IV V VI
VII VIII IX X

round – *v*, to change a number to the nearest whole number or the nearest number ending in zero

row – *n*, a series of people or things arranged in a straight line

S

scale – *n*, a device that is used for weighing people or things

score – *n*, the number of points in a game or sport

segment – *n*, a separate part of anything

sequence – *n*, a group of things that come one after the other

shape – *n*, the outer form of something

similarity – *n*, a comparable aspect

size – *n*, the extent to which something is large or small

square – *n*, a shape with four straight sides of equal length

strategy – *n*, a carefully planned way of doing something

subtract – *v*, to take one quantity or number away from another to find the remainder

switch – *v*, to replace one object with another

symbol – *n*, a picture or shape used to represent something

T

term – *n*, a number or figure in a sequence

2,214 → 2,221 → 2,228 → 2,235 → 2,242

times – *prep*, multiplied by

translation – *n*, the moving of a figure or shape from one position to another, without rotating, flipping, or changing anything else about it

twice – *adv*, two times the amount or rate of something

U

up – *adv*, from a lower to a higher place or position

V

value – *n*, the quantity or numerical amount of something

vertical – *adj*, going straight up or down from a level surface

Place Value Chart

Example: 34,253

TTh (ten thousands)	Th (thousands)	H (hundreds)	T (tens)	O (ones)
3	4	2	5	3

Math Symbols

addition	+
subtraction	–
greater than	>
less than	<
equal	=
multiplication	×

Cutout 1

Use on page 51 (**Unit 2**).

Multiplication Table

×	1	2	3	4	5	6	7	8	9	10
1	1	2	3	4	5	6	7	8	9	10
2	2	4	6	8	10	12	14	16	18	20
3	3	6	9	12	15	18	21	24	27	30
4	4	8	12	16	20	24	28	32	36	40
5	5	10	15	20	25	30	35	40	45	50
6	6	12	18	24	30	36	42	48	54	60
7	7	14	21	28	35	42	49	56	63	70
8	8	16	24	32	40	48	56	64	72	80
9	9	18	27	36	45	54	63	72	81	90
10	10	20	30	40	50	60	70	80	90	100

4. Mark the operations that represent the scales with a ✔.

a.

○ 22 +  = 34

○ 22 –  = 34

○ 34 +  = 22

b.

○ 3 +  = 19

○  – 3 = 19

○ 19 +  = 3

5. Solve the operations and write the unknown values.

a. △ – 33 = 15

△ = ☐

b. 36 + □ = 60

□ = ☐

Test 1 Study Page • Summary

Unit 1: Numbers and Patterns

Name: ______________________________ Grade: __________

Number Patterns

Numbers Up To 10,000

six thousand, two hundred thirteen 6,213

Counting

By 5s 1,311, 1,316, 1,321, 1,326, ...

By 10s 2,110, 2,120, 2,130, 2,140, ...

By 100s 6,100, 6,200, 6,300, 6,400, ...

Increasing and Decreasing Patterns

Pattern ⟶ + 2

Sequence ⟶ 32 ➡ 34 ➡ 36 ➡ 38

Number Patterns in a Hundreds Chart

There are patterns in the **diagonal**, **horizontal** and **vertical lines**.

1	2	3	4	5	6	7	8	9	10
11	12	13	14	15	16	17	18	19	20
21	22	23	24	25	26	27	28	29	30
31	32	33	34	35	36	37	38	39	40
41	42	43	44	45	46	47	48	49	50
51	52	53	54	55	56	57	58	59	60
61	62	63	64	65	66	67	68	69	70
71	72	73	74	75	76	77	78	79	80
81	82	83	84	85	86	87	88	89	90
91	92	93	94	95	96	97	98	99	100

Operations

Operations with One Unknown

$\triangle + 18 = 46$

$\triangle$ ↓ unknown value

$18 = 46$ known terms

Addition and Subtraction Operations with One Unknown

- Addition operations:

$\triangle + 18 = 46$

↓

$\triangle = 46 - 18$

$\triangle = 28$

- Subtraction operations:

$\triangle - 18 = 46$

↓

$\triangle = 46 + 18$

$\triangle = 64$

Test 1 Study Page • Review

Remove, answer, and glue in your notebook.

Unit 1: Numbers and Patterns

1. Write the word forms of the numbers.

a. 40,320 ▸ ____________________

b. 3,470 ▸ ____________________

c. 9,600 ▸ ____________________

d. 17,000 ▸ ____________________

2. Complete the counts.

a. By 100s

17,230, [ ], [ ], [ ]

b. By 10s

1,001, [ ], [ ], [ ]

3. Find the pattern for the number sequence.

[ ]

3,300 ➔ 3,350 ➔ 3,400 ➔ 3,450 ➔ 3,500

Test 2 Study Page • Review

Remove, answer, and glue in your notebook.

Unit 2: Multiplication

1. Count the elements by 4s and complete.

There are ________ groups of ________ .

There are ________ .

2. Write a multiplication operation for each representation.

a.

☐ × ☐ = ☐

b.

☐ × ☐ = ☐

Name: ______________________________ Grade: __________

Multiplication

Counting By 3s, 4s and 5s

	By 3s	By 4s	By 5s
Going forward	add 3	add 4	add 5
Going backward	subtract 3	subtract 4	subtract 5

Repeated Additon

Repeated addition is: $4 + 4 + 4 + 4 = 16$

$4 \times 4 = 16$

Equal Distribution

When you have **groups** with the **same number of elements**, you can find the total number of elements using **multiplication**.

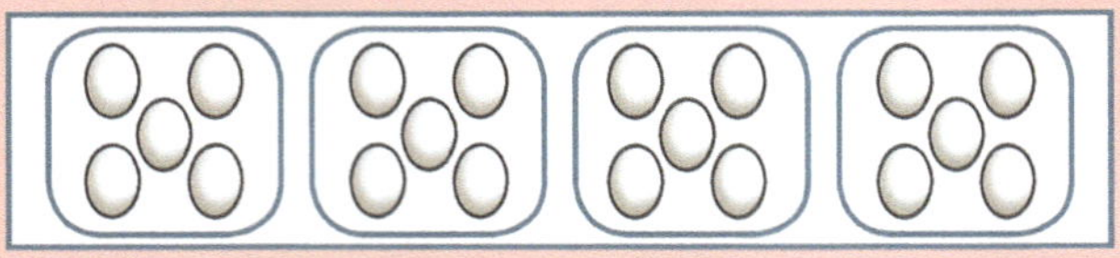

$5 + 5 + 5 + 5 = 20$

4 times 5 is 20

$4 \times 5 = 20$

One Corresponding to Many

When the elements of one group are equal in number to the elements of other groups, you can find the total number of elements in the other groups using multiplication.

1 day	2 days	3 days	4 days	5 days
6	12	18	24	30

Multiplication Word Problems

To solve a multiplication word problem that involves repetition of elements, follow these steps:

1. Identify the important information and the question.
2. Choose a multiplication strategy to answer the question.
3. Answer the question and then check your answer.

Test 2 Study Page • Summary

Unit 2: Multiplication

3. Read the problems and choose a multiplication strategy to solve them.

a. John is reading a book with twenty chapters. He wants to read four chapters a week. In how many weeks will he finish the book?

Answer: ______________________________

b. Lucy bought two notebooks for $7 each and a box of pencils for $5. If she pays with a $50 bill, how much change will she receive?

Answer: ______________________________

c. There are 32 bottles of soda in a box. If the bottles are in eight rows, how many columns will there be?

Answer: ______________________________

glue here
glue here
glue here
glue here
glue here

Test 3 Study Page • Review

Remove, answer, and glue in your notebook

Unit 3: Fractions and Location

1. Divide the shapes to represent the fractions. Then color them.

a. $\frac{3}{8}$ ▸

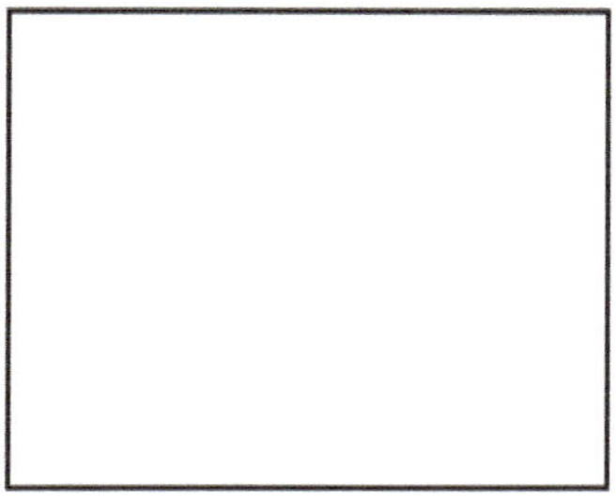

b. $\frac{2}{5}$ ▸

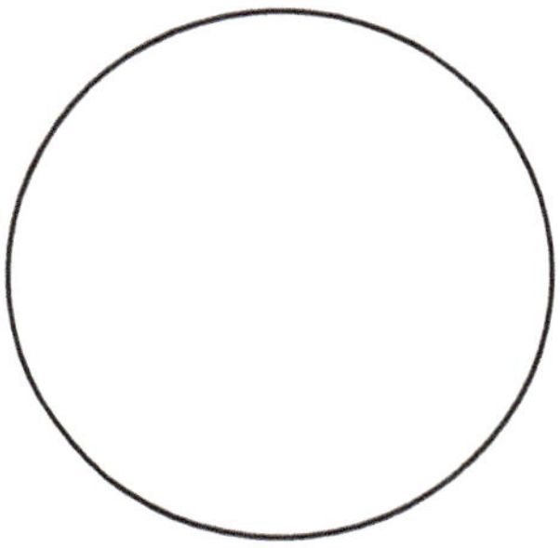

c. $\frac{5}{6}$ ▸

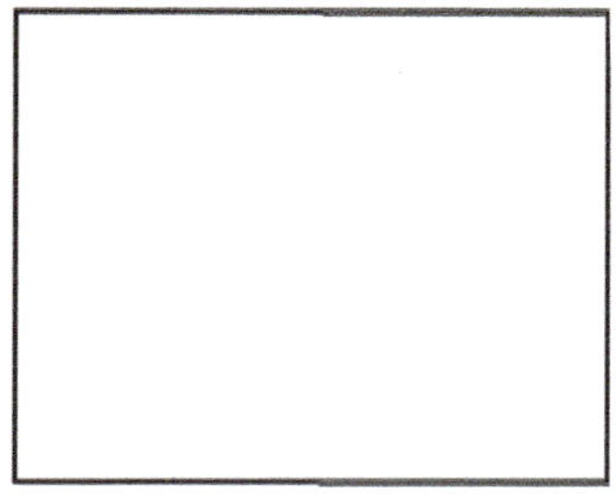

d. $\frac{4}{9}$ ▸

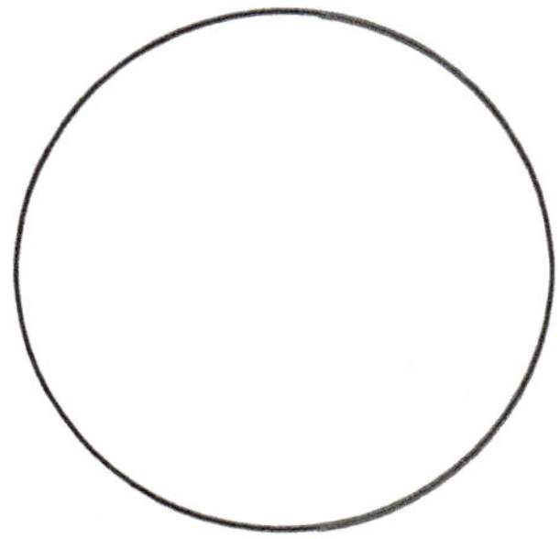

2. Write the fractions that the colored parts represent.

a.

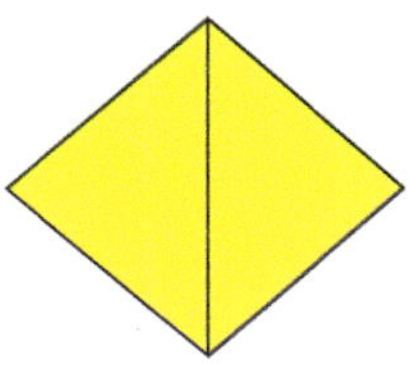 ▸ $\frac{\quad}{\quad}$

b.

 ▸ $\frac{\quad}{\quad}$

c.

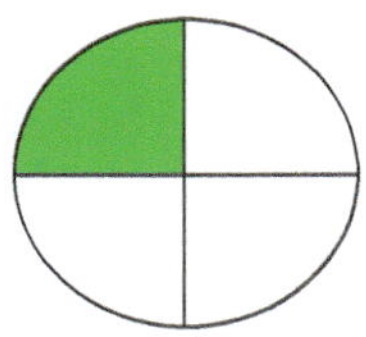 ▸ $\frac{\quad}{\quad}$

d.

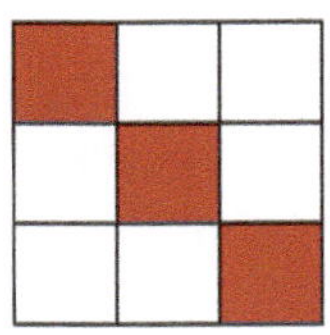 ▸ $\frac{\quad}{\quad}$

Name: ______________________________ Grade: ________

Fractions

The Whole and its Parts

$\frac{2}{6}$

2 → parts selected from the whole

6 → number of parts the whole is divided into

Terms of a Fraction

$\frac{1}{4}$

1 → **numerator**

— → **fraction bar**

4 → **denominator**

Reading Fractions

First, you read the **numerator**. Then the **denominator** is read as an ordinal number. For example:

$\frac{1}{2}$ **one-half**, $\frac{3}{4}$ **three-fourths**, $\frac{5}{6}$ **five-sixths**

Location

Location on a Map

To describe a location on a map, you can use **points of reference** and **positions**: above, below, to the left or to the right.

The hospital is to the right of the park. The supermarket is between the school and the market.

Location on a Grid

To describe a location on a grid, identify a **point of reference** and count the squares between the positions. You can also use **coordinates**.

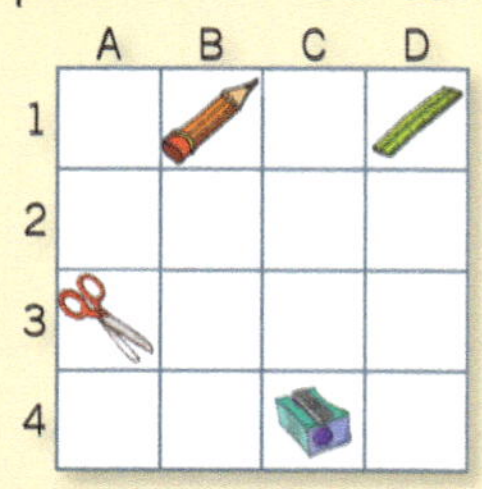

The pencil is located in B1.

The pencil is located two squares to the left of the ruler.

Translation on a Grid

A translation changes the location of something on a map or grid, but it does not change its shape or size.

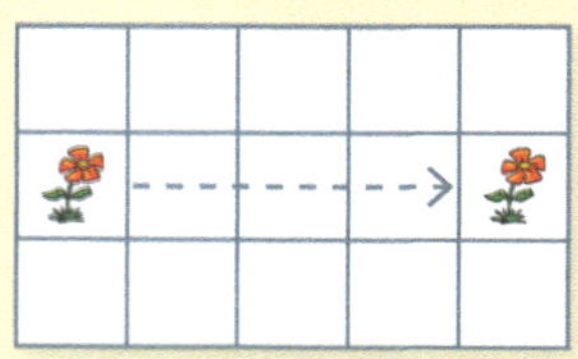

Test 3 Study Page • Summary

Unit 3: Fractions and Location

3. Look at the map and complete the sentences.

Anna's bedroom is ______________________________

The parent's bedroom is ______________________________

The kitchen is ______________________________

4. Read the instructions and translate the arrows in the grids.

a. Move the arrow two squares to the right and three squares down.

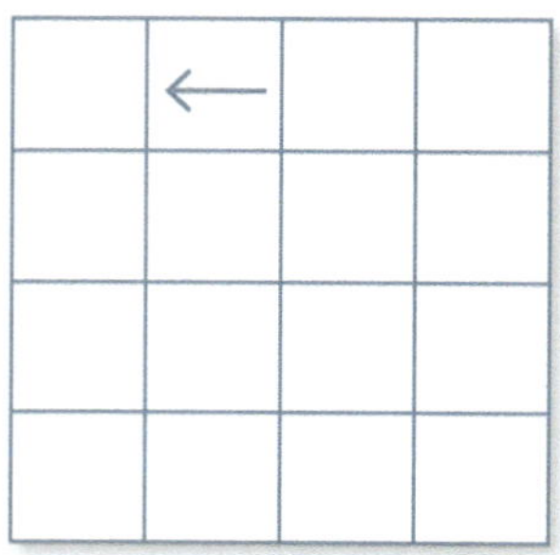

b. Move the arrow three squares to the left and one square up.

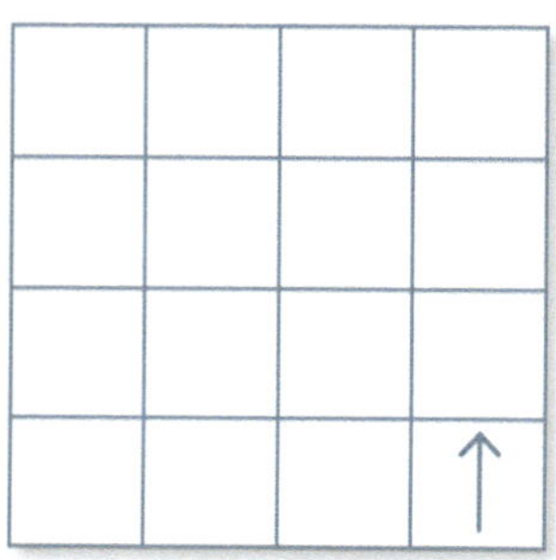

Test 4 Study Page • Review

Remove, answer, and glue in your notebook.

Unit 4: Numbers and Time

1. Look at the numbers and complete the table according to the digits in red.

	Number	Position	Place Value	Decomposition of Number
a.	90,300			
b.	7,803			
c.	12,874			

2. Mark the number that is bigger than the first number with a check ✔ and the number that is smaller with a cross ✘.

a. 5,320

- ◯ 5,230
- ◯ 5,320
- ◯ 5,420

b. 10,000

- ◯ 9,000
- ◯ 99,000
- ◯ 10,000

c. 22,684

- ◯ 22,674
- ◯ 22,774
- ◯ 22,684

3. Put the numbers in order on the number line.

12,315, 12,325, 12,310, 12,320

Name: ______________________________ Grade: __________

Numbers

Composing and Decomposing

Th	H	T	O	→ place
3	4	2	1	
↓	↓	↓	↓	
3,000	400	20	1	→ place value

Comparing and Putting in Order

- Using a place value chart

Th	H	T	O
6	9	3	0

>

Th	H	T	O
6	9	0	3

- Using a number line

3,652 < 3,662 < 3,672 < 3,682

Rounding

	Number	**32,679**
Rounding	to the nearest ten	32,680
	to the nearest hundred	32,700
	to the nearest thousand	33,000
	to the nearest ten thousand	30,000

Time

Calendars

Timelines

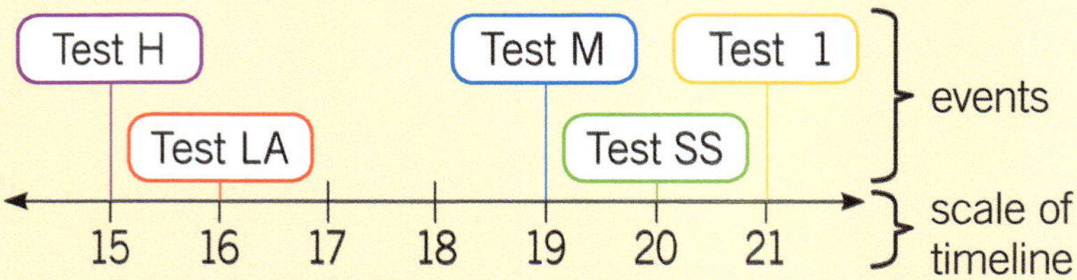

Digital and Analog Clocks

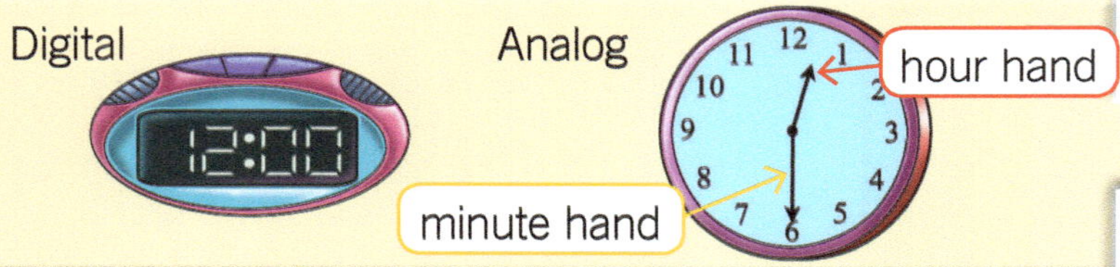

Test 4 Study Page • Summary

Unit 4: Numbers and Time

4. Look at the calendar and answer.

September 2019						
M	T	W	T	F	S	S
						1
2	3	4	5	6	7	8
9	10	11	12	13	14	15
16	17	18	19	20	21	22
23	24	25	26	27	28	29
30						

a. What date is the Saturday before September 1st?

____

b. What date is the Tuesday after September 17th?

____

c. Joshua turned in the first part of his project on September 3rd. The second part needs to be in 10 days later. On what date will he turn in the second part?

____

d. How many weeks does this month have? ____________________

e. Alex goes to the gym on Monday, Tuesday and Friday. How many days will she go to the gym in September?

____

5. Draw the time on the analog clocks to match the time on the digital clocks.

a.

b.

c.

glue here

glue here

glue here

glue here

glue here

Test 5 Study Page • Review

Remove, answer, and glue in your notebook.

Unit 5: Surveys and Data

1. Analyze the information and answer.

My Favorite Dessert	
Dessert	**Votes**
Pudding	6
Ice Cream	2
Jello	5

a. Represent the information in a bar chart.

b. Which is the most popular dessert among the people surveyed?

____

c. What is the variation between most and least favorite desserts?

____

Name: ______________________ Grade: __________

Surveys, Tables and Charts

Making Pictographs and Bar Charts

Surveys

Surveys help you to **collect data** or the opinions of people by asking them simple **questions**.

Tables, Bar Charts and Pictographs

Tables, bar charts and pictographs help you to **organize** and **analyze** data.

Favorite Color	
Color	**Votes**
Yellow	2
Green	1
Red	5
Blue	4

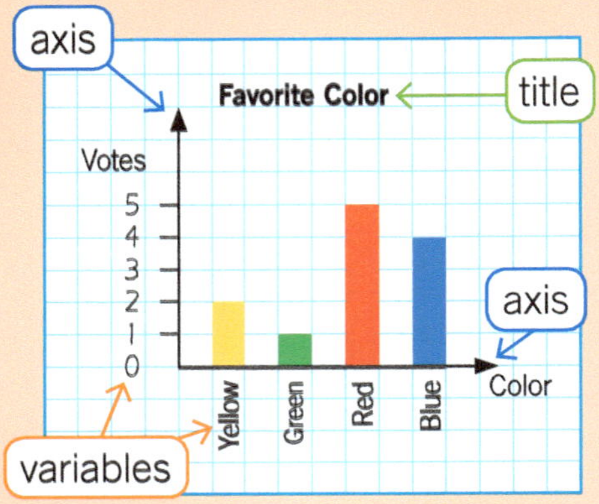

Pictographs and Bar Charts With Scales

Scales are used to represent data more easily. In pictographs, the scale is represented with symbols, and in bar graphs it is represented on the axes.

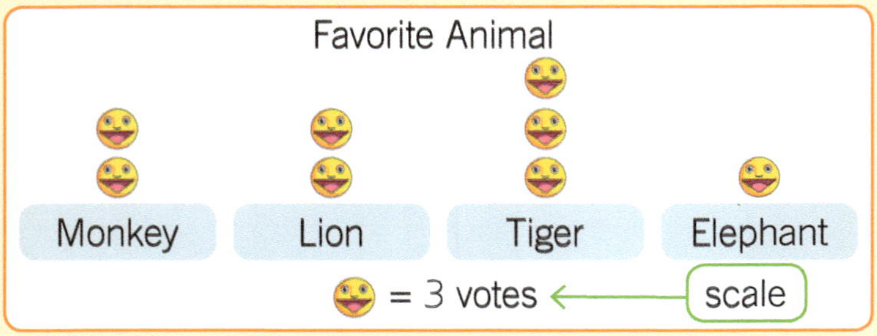

Test 5 Study Page • Summary

Unit 5: Surveys and Data

2. Look at the pictograph and answer.

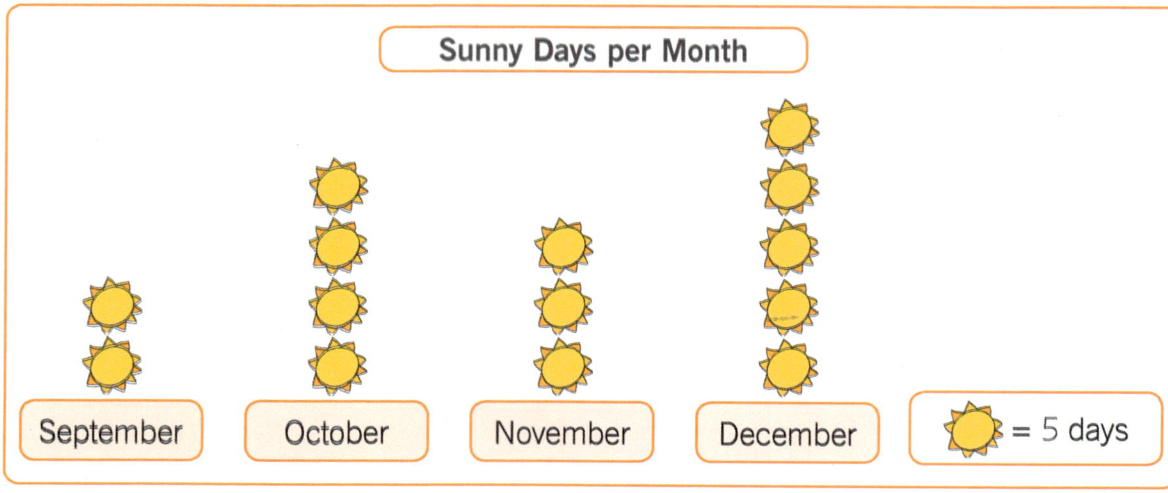

a. What information does the pictograph show?

____

____

b. Explain the scale of the pictograph.

____

c. Which month had the most sunny days? Which had the fewest?

____

d. How many sunny days were there in October?

____

e. How many sunny days were there, in total, in the four months?

____